Break EVERY Stinking CHAIN!

Healing For Hidden Wounds

Denice Colson, PhD

Published by TraumaEducation.com

Privacy: To protect the privacy of people mentioned in this book, I have changed names and identifying information, with the exception being myself.

Biblical passages: Unless otherwise indicated, all Scripture quotations are taken from the Holy Bible, New Living Translation, copyright © 1996, 2004, 2007, 2013, 2015 by Tyndale House Foundation. Used by permission of Tyndale House Publishers, Inc., Carol Stream, Illinois 60188. All rights reserved.

Inspiration: While the 12 numbered sentences, identified as "12 Strategic Stages," were inspired by the Twelve Steps of A.A., they are not really an adaptation. Rather, they were created specifically for this program, and should not be construed otherwise. A.A., which is a program concerned only with recovery from alcoholism, is not in any way affiliated with this program.

Disclaimer: This information is intended for general information only. No warranties or guarantees of any kind are expressed or implied by the author or publisher. Every effort has been made to provide accurate and complete information. By reading this material, the reader agrees that the author and publisher are NOT responsible for any loss incurred resulting from the information contained in this publication. The reader is responsible for his or her own actions. This is not medical or psychological treatment but predominantly spiritual in nature.

DEDICATION

God for His love, His faithfulness, His inspiration to write this book, and most of all His salvation.

My parents for your faithfulness to God and prayers for me, even before my birth.

My husband and daughters for your patience and willingness to deal with all of my crazy ideas and believing in the Spirit inside me.

The staff at Eagle's Landing Christian Counseling Center: Thanks for your partnership, your faithfulness, and your willingness to join with me in this ministry to hurting people. Thanks for your patience, editing (Christyn and Kimberly), feedback, and willingness to use this material with wounded clients.

My pastor, Tim Dowdy and the staff of Eagle's Landing First Baptist Church: for your encouragement to write and to follow the path that God has put before me. I'd list all of your names, if I could!

All the others who have contributed to this book THANK YOU! Your encouragement means more to me than I can say.

PREFACE

Since 1982, I have been helping people who struggle with depression, anxiety, anger, fear, and low self-esteem. Around 1992 I began to realize that what most of my clients had in common was unresolved emotional and psychological injuries, some more shocking than others were. Many of the wounds took place in childhood or adolescence, and some in a previous adult relationship. In most of the cases, however, the pain was clearly still affecting him or her, even if he or she wasn't dwelling on it all the time. Around this time, a fellow counselor introduced me to the idea that I needed to address past trauma directly using structure rather than just treating symptoms like depression, anxiety, and anger. Building on this foundation, I began my journey to bring Biblical truth and psychological research together to help people be free from the past wounds that keep them chained, bound, and effectively sidelined from living the life they wanted to live.

I've written this book because I long for YOU to be free from the chains of trauma, too! I yearn for you to move through the healing process and not stay stuck in your pain! I know it can be done because I've done it and I've walked with others through healing from incredibly horrific experiences. You too can break the chains of past trauma! Stop living a life controlled by past pain and start living the life of *freedom you long for!*

CONTENTS

LET THE HEALING BEGIN!

To all the souls that are hurting, God will bring you grace.

To all the souls that are searching, God will show His face.

To all the souls feeling trapped, freedom will soon come.

To all the souls who've lost their map, the Spirit will bring a new one.

His face, His hands, His feet, His heart we are all designed to know.

His lap, His hug, His laugh, His caress we can all begin to show.

Join the movement; join the song of freedom from our pain.

It's Christ who's come, it's He who was slain to break EVERY Stinking Chain!

Denice Adcock Colson

INTRODUCTION

FREEDOM. We all want it, expect it, and even demand it. You're probably free on the outside to come and go as you please, but inside you might feel trapped in a personal jail of depression, anger, anxiety or fear. Feeling *chained* to past wounds, recurring negative thoughts or relationships will keep you feeling *stuck* and inhibit that sense of freedom you crave. While in your head you believe that Christ brings freedom and that a relationship with God is the answer, you continue to struggle with aligning your emotions with this truth.

There are several myths that have been passed around in the Christian church—the Body of Christ---about emotions, psychological wounds, and treatment for mental health issues. Many Christians have been afraid of psychology and counseling, believing that the application of psychological principles is always *against* God and *against* faith in Christ. In fact, some Christians still believe that any use of psychological training, research or counsel is heresy and should never be used! These same people, however, go to see medical doctors when they are sick, take antibiotics when they have an infection, and allow non-Christian doctors trained in secular medical schools to operate on them. This attitude has confused and frustrated me.

"Science is thinking God's thoughts after Him,"[1] according to Johannes Kepler, the father of modern astronomy, a trained Lutheran minister and scientist born in 1571. He solved the problem of Mars (the fact that Mars appeared to move backward across the sky) and correctly identified that planets travel in elliptical orbits around the

Sun and not in circular orbits around the Earth. He and most great scientists at the time believed that God designed everything for us to be curious about, to study, and to try to understand. The false idea that Biblical truth and science were two opposite things was foreign to these great scientists. Now, a growing group of Christian mental health providers agrees that all truth is God's truth, and we are fighting back against this false dichotomy. Many great Christian theologians concur, including Augustine, Thomas Aquinus, John Calvin[2], and a modern theologian, Gaeblin[3]. Remaining curious and attempting to *understand* how the universe works is our *responsibility* and a way of honoring God. That's what the integration of psychology and theology is all about.

Additionally, psychologists are recognizing the importance of treating the whole person and including spirituality in the mix. Spiritually conscious psychological care has become the minimum expected by the American Psychological Association. Spiritually avoidant care used to be the norm, and with many professional mental health workers, it continues to be. However, there is a growing movement to stop this unethical treatment.[4]

Psychology is the scientific study of human behavior. While it is true that all bad human behavior is ultimately attributable to our sin nature, specific human behavior requires specific explanations. Why do true Christ-believers still struggle with recurring interpersonal issues and even experience family splits and divorce?[5] Why do famous and Godly theologians suffer from depression,[6] hidden addictions, and even commit suicide?[7] Why do Christians get divorced? Why do children who grow up in Christian families hate God or dismiss Him as adults? Some of the research on Christians and divorce or other family and health issues has been exaggerated and misreported.[8] However, as a veteran listener to the stories of demoralized people, what they all have in common, regardless of their religious views or faith is unhealed emotional and psychological wounds. Remarkably, many very intelligent and Godly people are oblivious to the fact that these past wounds are the source of their current emotional, psychological, spiritual, relational and even physical problems. Perhaps you too have bought the myth which I will address in chapter one, "If it happened when I was a child, it doesn't affect me anymore." This is not true, and it's impossible! (Unless of course you received a brain transplant.) In chapter 1 I will present compelling research to support the fact that it *does* affect you—even 50 or more years later, and will impact you for the rest of your life But wait, there is hope for healing!

You might be asking yourself, *"How did I get here? I thought the past was in the past."* In chapter two, I'll introduce you to The Trauma Survivor Blueprint©, a six-stage process that explains how we go from wound to survivor, and become stuck repeating the same negative behaviors. I'll also introduce you to a plan for healing, The Three Phases of Strategic Trauma and Abuse Recovery©. While this plan will assist you on your path to healing, it's important to remember that this type of transformation takes time. It's a process. Salvation is immediate, but transformation occurs slowly and over time. I think that what we call transformation is also the process of HEALING. In other words, healing from trauma is the means through which God transforms us. This means identifying the wounds in your life and allowing God to heal them from the inside out. It is a different approach to change. Rather than changing from the outside in, you are embracing your weakness and inner-wounds, and allowing God to do the changing from the inside out. One participant in the class on which this book is based wrote, *"For the first time in ten years of marriage, and almost thirty years of silence, I have begun to initiate conversations with my husband, family, friends and most importantly with God-about the trauma that has occurred in my life. My faith has begun to build slowly and I have learned the value of starting simply, which Dr. Colson so aptly teaches. As my faith grows, so does my hope. My hope to you, dear reader, is that you will experience the same."*

This book introduces you to a 12-stage process that gives you a roadmap to follow. Think of it like a GPS for moving through healing from emotional wounds. It will help you know where you are, and guide you to where you want to be. Chapters three through six will provide a breakdown of the first phase of recovery and address the individual steps needed to begin your healing journey. Using psychological research and Biblical interpretation, we will look at five additional myths about trauma that have infiltrated society and the Christian church and disprove each. In chapter seven, I will introduce you to the next phase of recovery and provide evidence as to why you should continue. Of course, it is your choice as to whether you go deeper or stop here.

You can be free from the hidden chains of past wounds. God can heal the wounds of trauma. You don't have to live with overwhelming depression, anxiety, fear, or anger. It doesn't matter the size of the wound, any size wound hurts. Recently, my youngest daughter had a root canal. I was in more pain watching than she was; she didn't complain at all, before or after the procedure. In contrast, a few days before her root canal, my husband got some tiny cuts on his fingers, and he had to wear bandages on them for several days because the pain was so bad. It's not the size of your wound, it's the *location.* When that location is inside of you, it hurts, no matter how "tiny" it might look from the outside. Don't dismiss your particular kind of wound because it's not as dramatic as someone else's. It still affects you and God still wants to heal it!

MORE ABOUT INTEGRATING PSYCHOLOGY AND THE BIBLE

The Bible is the single most important book ever written. It is God's Word. It has transformed the world, and it connects us to the most important person ever born on this Earth, Jesus Christ. It tells us who He is, how He relates to people, and the basic nature and history of human beings. The Bible tells us how we can have a relationship with God, the creator of all things, through Jesus Christ.

As I mentioned earlier, psychology is the scientific study of human behavior. Just like biology, chemistry, and physics are the study of natural laws and how to apply them through medicine or engineering, psychology is an attempt to understand why people behave the way they do and how to change bad behavior into better behavior. Mental Health treatment is the application of psychology, much as medicine is the application of biology, chemistry, and physiology. *Without the foundation of the Bible, however, mental health treatment has no anchor, no foundational principles.* If the purpose of applying psychology is to change human behavior, but everything is relative and there are no moral absolutes, then who determines what "bad" behavior is and why one behavior is "better" than another is? Psychology doesn't have an answer for that. The best they can come up with is that better behavior makes you feel better, improves relationships, and makes society more functional.

The problem with that is, societal norms, the rules about what is acceptable behavior and what isn't, are continually changing. For example, in ancient Greece, ritualistic kidnapping of young teen boys and sexual liaisons initiated by an adult man with younger teen boys was commonplace and even encouraged by the boys' father.[9] In addition, rulers kept children of the same or opposite sex as sexual toys. In our modern society, this behavior is widely condemned and illegal. Men and women who behave this way now are considered pedophiles and put in prison to protect the rest of society from their destructive behavior. Incidentally, there are people who are trying to make this type of relationship between adults and minors acceptable again. In fact, the sexual exploitation and sexual enslavement of children, also called "trafficking," is actually gaining popularity,[10] rather than decreasing. There really is nothing new under the sun! People treat each other horribly and have since Cain murdered his brother Able.

The Bible does contain the answers to societal and individual problems. I think it is unfortunate, however, that the Church seems to focus "out there somewhere," but overlook the adults and children living in our own communities who experience abuse, exploitation, and even neglect in less obvious ways. Unfortunately, it has become commonplace in the church to, on the one hand, acknowledge the impact of something like human trafficking, but on the other hand, give the impression that divorce is something people should "just get over." People also get the impression that not feeling loved by a parent or parents, or growing up with an alcoholic parent, or with a screaming parent, is something that we should just forget about and overcome. You may consider these life situations as small boulders in your path that you should be able to climb over easily. Leaving the impression that these type of life situations are inconvenient and annoying, but no big deal. Instead of embracing people, we tend to judge them for their survival choices, like feeling sorry for themselves, using drugs and alcohol, sexual misconduct, inability to work, etc., rather than choosing to empathize with their pain and loss.

These "smaller" wounds that many people experience are the very things that our enemy uses to devalue our faith, limit our growth, and block our roots from growing down deeper into Christ (Col 2:7-9). (Can your roots ever be *too* deep into Christ?) Many well-meaning church leaders have encouraged Christians to ignore these, to "just put them under the blood," overcome them, or forget about them and focus on Christ, but this has only enabled the enemy to portray the Church/Body of Christ as unsympathetic and uncaring, and has contributed to shrinking the local church. At one conference I attended, a very compelling speaker instructed us to pretend we were at the airport and imagine taking our baggage to the handler (Jesus) and walking away. "It's that easy!" she assured us. GIVE ME A BREAK! Give yourself a break! For most of us, it is just not that simple, and telling us it *should* be easy only leads to increase our guilt, shame, and sense of inadequacy, further alienating us from the Body of Christ.

While we (Christians) will go out and demonstrate our love by bringing food and water to other countries, we probably don't know the pain the person sitting next to us in church has had to endure. We don't know why they don't smile or won't shake hands, hold hands during prayer time, avoid eye contact, seem rude and aloof, or use drugs, drink, or whatever. I hope this type of isolation in the Body of Christ can end so that real revival can happen again! I mean REAL, exploding, outpouring, and insanely inspiring revival.

What would happen in your church if people bore each other's burdens, as Christ commands us to do? How would your relationships change if you sincerely demonstrated interest in other's burdens, without judgement, and were willing to share your own burdens? Both listening and sharing require the choice of vulnerability. It also requires us to identify the roots of our burdens—unhealed wounds—and begin to let God heal us in community with others, just like Paul talked about in Galatians 6. This book is my attempt at helping to initiate, support, and bring some organization to that healing conversation.

While salvation through Christ is what leads to immediate freedom from sin, transformation is an ongoing process. This book is part of the transformation process and seeks to meet you wherever you are. You may be wondering if God even exists and if He does exist whether or not He even cares about you and your personal circumstances. On the other hand, you may be a Christian ministry leader, active in the church for years, leading others to Christ, praying, reading your Bible daily, but still find yourself stuck in emotional quicksand and not knowing where to turn for help. Whether you find yourself at either extreme or anywhere in between, this book and its guiding principles will help you move forward in the process of healing from the wounds that are keeping you stuck. *Are you ready to heal? Let's get started!*

CHAPTER 1:
UNCOVERING
HIDDEN WOUNDS

"Mental pain is less dramatic than physical pain, but it is more common and also more hard to bear. The frequent attempt to conceal mental pain increases the burden: it is easier to say 'My tooth is aching' than to say 'My heart is broken.'"

C.S. Lewis

When I was 14 years old, I was living with my family in Piper, Kansas, which is a small suburb of Kansas City. It was 1974, the year that President Richard M. Nixon resigned from office. We didn't have a VCR then, only a tape recorder. I was home alone and wanted to record the live news report of President Nixon's famous resignation announcement and exit from the White House. I used my little tape recorder and sat in front of the television holding it up to the speaker. After a while, I really needed to use the bathroom. When a commercial break came, I turned off the recorder and ran into the bathroom. I was in such a hurry to get back to the television, that I missed clearing the doorway by just a fraction of an inch. Unfortunately, that fraction of an inch was enough to catch my pinky toe on the doorstop. I screamed, and jumped around on one foot. I was in excruciating pain! I was dedicated, though, and while holding my foot, I turned on the recorder to get the rest of the proceedings. Later, my parents took me to have it x-rayed and, sure enough, it was broken. On the surface, I couldn't tell it was broken, but the pain certainly told me something was wrong. Because the wound was beneath the surface, I had to have an x-ray to know that my foot was broken.

Hidden wounds, wounds deep beneath the surface can cause a lot of pain on the surface, and in our society, we have a major problem with pain—both physical and emotional. Addiction to pain medication has become such a major problem that one Oxycodone pill is so expensive on the black-market that it's currently cheaper to buy Heroin. Emotional pain and physical pain are connected, and the brain responds to both similarly, demanding action to alleviate it. However, for many people, the source of the pain remains hidden beneath shame, guilt, and fear.

Taking something to deal with the emotional pain works, temporarily. However, the answer to the problem of pain is not NO pain. The absence of pain can be a problem in itself. One addiction counselor said, "Trauma is the problem, substance use is the solution until the solution becomes the problem" (unknown). Numbing pain has a similar impact to the disease of leprosy. Leprosy, a mildly contagious disease now mostly restricted to tropical Africa and Asia, affects the skin, mucous membranes, and eventually the nerve endings.[11] Brand and Yancy write, "Leprous people live a virtually pain-free existence. Many of us would do anything to live a pain-free life. Yet in fact, the absence of pain is the greatest enemy of the leper. Again and again they wound and impale themselves. Yet they don't feel a thing."[12] The purpose of physical pain is to warn you about damage or potential damage to your body that needs your attention. When we don't have pain, it's not that the damage doesn't occur, we just don't feel it. Therefore, we don't do anything about it.

Psychological and emotional pain is similar to physical pain in that it demands a response. While a physical wound is visible, emotional wounds aren't because they strike beneath the surface, affecting your inner-most identity. When a physical wound is pervasive enough, we call it trauma and take people to the emergency room. When emotional and psychological wounds are pervasive enough, we also call them "trauma". However, we frequently hide these wounds; bury them deep in our memories where we hide them from others and ourselves beneath fear, guilt, and shame. Dr. Vincent Felitti, a physician, researcher, and one of the co-founders of the Adverse Childhood Experiences Study points out that, when it comes to emotional or psychological trauma, time does not heal, it conceals.[13] However, similar to the experience of a leper, when emotional wounds go unattended or intentionally ignored, the wound spreads, affecting more and more of your mind, emotions, and even your spirit.

DEFINING TRAUMA

Trauma, whether physical, psychological or emotional, creates pain and demands action. The word "trauma" comes from the Greek word that means an injury or wound. Psychological trauma is a wound also, but to the inside of you, your identity. The term "traumatic stress", as in "Post-Traumatic Stress" is the demand for action in the brain that comes out of the experience.[14] When you are physically bleeding, the action you take is obvious. You try to stop it! Alternatively, you may pass out. If someone sees you bleeding, he/she may take matters into their own hands and do something about it. When it comes to emotional bleeding, however, your responses may be concealed or your response may be even to conceal your pain. The quote by C.S. Lewis, which I used at the beginning of the chapter, is so true: "Mental pain is less dramatic than physical pain, but it is more common and also more hard to bear. The frequent attempt to conceal mental pain increases the burden: it is easier to say "My tooth is aching" than to say "My heart is broken."[15]

Your brain doesn't seem to distinguish between physical and emotional pain. Pain is pain, and most of the chemical responses, fight, flight, fright or freeze, are the same. In addition, there's a universal expectation we humans have about pain...it SHOULDN'T happen, ever! Thus, we find ourselves spending an excessive amount of money on pain medications, prescription and non-prescription drugs, alcohol, antidepressants and anti-anxiety medicines to deal with not only physical pain, but also emotional pain.

We label many different kinds of events as traumatic. Some events that people have considered traumatic include: physical abuse, sexual abuse, physical neglect, emotional abuse, emotional neglect, death of a loved one, domestic violence, living with an alcoholic or drug addict/abuse, living with someone with a mental illness, having a mental illness, growing up poor and hungry, rape, a parent never telling you they love you, death of a pet, threatened killing of a pet, family member in prison, family member in combat, being in combat, abandoned by a parent or a spouse, screamed at, called names, or watching someone else be abused. This is not a complete list, by any means! Later, as we talk about what makes an event traumatic, this list will grow quite a bit.

TRAUMA MYTH #1

I will be confronting and discussing six myths people hold regarding trauma and it's healing throughout this book. These are myths I've come across while counseling trauma survivors as well as training other counselors to work with trauma survivors. Not everyone believes all of the myths, and you may not agree that they are myths. You may think they are true statements. These myths are thoughts and beliefs that, while they may actually have a kernel of truth in them, overall they are untrue when it comes to their application to psychological trauma. Some of them are urban legends that are passed down as ways to cope with pain or explain away something. They may be unspoken beliefs that protect people from reality that is painful and hard to bear. They may also be thought of as assumptions people make that haven't been voiced or really thought through. These myths are important to call out and challenge because they block people from healing from trauma or from even identifying the source of their wounds. Even if you don't agree, be open minded as you read about each thought and the information supporting its being considered a myth.

Myth #1 is, "If it happened when I was a child, it doesn't affect me anymore." This is the most common myth I hear. However, it isn't true! Let's consider the facts, then you decide for yourself.

Research shows that 61% of men and 51% of women surveyed in the general population report experiencing at least one trauma in their lifetime.[16] In addition, 59% of men and women report experiencing at least one Adverse Childhood Experience (ACE) in their lifetime, and 9% experience 5 or more ACE.[17] So, how do you know if it's still affecting you? You may think, "That happened so long ago it doesn't bother me anymore!" Actually, what research shows is that traumatic events that happen especially in childhood will still affect us even 50 or more years later. Why? Because it affects your brain, changes the actual wiring in your brain and therefore it affects your body, your mind and your spirit. It affects us not only directly, but changes the way we see ourselves and the world around us, how we experience relationships and, most importantly, how we view and experience God. Wherever you go, you take your brain with you.

Think about this example: Paulo grows up in Brazil and Paul grows up in Georgia. Both Paulo and Paul are born not speaking, not walking, not doing anything but crying. Because Paulo's parents speak Portuguese, he learns to speak Portuguese; because his family lives in a rural environment, he learns to ride horses, to plant and harvest his food. Because Paul's parents speak English with a southern accent, Paul learns to speak English with a southern accent; because his family lives in the suburbs of a large city, he learns to ride in cars everywhere, to ride motorcycles, to play football, to go to the grocery store and Chick-fil-a to buy food. These experiences shape the way he sees himself and how he sees the world around him. If Paulo grows up with an alcoholic father who goes into rages, what will that teach him about the world? If Paul grows up with loving parents until age 10, but then they suddenly get divorced, what will that teach him about the world?

Of all these lessons learned, which ones will they forget? When will Paulo suddenly forget Portuguese and start speaking English or Paul suddenly forget English and start speaking Portuguese? NEVER! Both boys learn only what they were taught and personally experienced. You learn what you live, and you live what you learn because your brain is recording your experiences.

Your brain is like a super-computer. Even though you can only see a few things on the screen, there are lots of programs running in the background that influence what you see and what you are able to do. In addition, God has wired us with some specific expectations about life and when these expectations aren't met, not only do we grieve these contradicted expectations, but we adapt and change the way we develop, the decisions we make, and how we experience relationships, including God. Just because you don't repeat the same exact pattern doesn't mean it's not affecting you, especially when the damage is on the inside. There isn't an x-ray machine to use on your identity in order to tell if something got broken, like with my toe.

In a research project called "The Still-Face Experiment"[18], the research asked a mother to interact with her 18-month-old child. In the video, the baby is happy, babbling, talking and interacting with the mother in a warm and happy way. Then the researcher asked the mom to turn away for just a second and, when she turns back, not to respond to the baby. She didn't leave the room or move away, but kept a blank expression on her face without responding to the baby's attempts to interact. You can see by the baby's reaction that she notices it right away. In the 2 minutes the mother doesn't respond, the baby reaches out with both hands pleading with the mother. She shrieks very loud, she loses control of her posture and begins to cry. When the mother starts responding again, the baby goes back to interacting. Other researchers have repeated this experiment multiple times with the same results. It demonstrates that, even at this young age, God wired us for interaction and connection. When we don't get that, even for a short while, it affects us emotionally, psychologically, and even physically. Imagine what would happen if the mother continued this for hours or even days. The impact would change the baby's behavior in more permanent ways. Traumatic experiences disconnect us, interfere with our attachments, and trigger grief.

The Impact of Childhood Adversity

Another ongoing research project called the Adverse Childhood Experiences Study started in 1995 and is collecting data on 17,000+ middle-class Americans from San Diego, California. The researchers looked at 10 types of childhood adversity including sexual abuse, physical abuse and neglect, psychological abuse and neglect, loss of a biological parent (to death, divorce or abandonment), alcohol or drug abuse in the home, a family member going to prison, mother being treated violently, and depression or mental illness in the home. Of those surveyed, 2/3rds had at least one source of adversity and one in fourteen had an ACE "score" (zero-ten possible) of four or more.[19] Since it started, and as of the writing of this book, the principal investigators, Dr. Vincent Felitti and Dr. Robert Anda, have published 61 research papers that are available at CDC.gov. Researchers replicated this study in 20 US states and Puerto Rico as well as China, Macedonia, Philippines, Saudi Arabia, South Africa, Thailand, and Vietnam. As of the writing of this book, people have completed ACE surveys in Albania, Latvia, Lithuania, and Macedonia, with further studies underway in Montenegro, Romania, Russian Federation and Turkey all with the same general results.[20] In fact, some show an even stronger link than the original study.

This research demonstrates a very clear link between childhood trauma and adult addiction, depression, anxiety, obesity, homelessness, unemployment, domestic violence, sexually transmitted diseases, teen pregnancy, elective abortion, and suicide attempts in addition to COPD, cancer, liver disease, and a 20-year decrease in life expectancy.

THE ACE PYRAMID

The ACE researchers have diagramed their outcomes in the shape of a pyramid. The pyramid shape illustrates the nature of the connections between childhood adversity and the multiple layers of impact. Adverse Childhood At the base of the pyramid are ACE experiences. We'll call this level one. As we move upward, each subsequent level is slightly smaller, demonstrating that, while each level clearly builds on the previous levels, not everyone makes this journey up the pyramid. However, as the number of adverse experiences increases, the more likely a person is to develop the symptoms, or move up the pyramid. Let's look at each level individually. We've already discussed the first level, Adverse Childhood Experiences. They are the ten types of childhood adversity studied by the researchers.

Level 2: Interrupted brain development. People who have experienced childhood adversity show signs of interrupted brain development, shown in level two of the pyramid. What this means is that research shows decreased neuro-connections between the frontal cortex and the rest of the brain, as well as decreased development in various parts of the brain, including the hippocampus, which is responsible for sequencing of events and other memories.[21] When you are born, your brain is very plastic. Organization has already begun even before birth, and your mother's physical and emotional state affects this first bit of organization. As you begin to interact with the outside world, your brain begins to organize itself further, and this continues throughout your entire life. The first years are very important because they build brain architecture. During these early years, researchers estimate that new connections between neurons, that is, brain nerve cells, are forming at a rate of 700-1000 per second! Think of building a house; first, the builder lays the foundation, then the posts and beams go up, then the walls and the roof. Each new experience builds on your previous experiences.

Because traumatic experiences like those listed above raise the stress level from positive or tolerable to toxic, the stress hormones created interfere with healthy brain development, weakening connections in the brain. Additional research on toxic stress and the brain by Dr. Bremner shows that military veterans diagnosed with PTSD have smaller hippocampi.[22] Many other researchers have found the same result. What this means is that there are less connections and less integration in this part of the brain than in others. Research makes it very clear that toxic stress damages the brain whether it happens to the person as a child or an adult. The difference is, during childhood, the foundation of brain architecture is forming and the brain will build all future learning on this foundation.

Level 3: Social, emotional, and psychological problems. Interrupted brain development, or at least altered development, leads to social, emotional, psychological and spiritual problems.[23] While the ACE study does not address spirituality, I've included it here because other studies have considered the impact of childhood trauma on spiritual development. Examples of issues at this level include, adults with an ACE score of four or more were 460% more likely to be suffering from depression. The likelihood of adult suicide attempts increased 30-fold, or 3,000%, with an ACE score of 7 or more. Childhood and adolescent suicide attempts increased 51-fold, or 5,100%, with an ACE score of 7 or more. Research outside of the ACE study links childhood trauma to spiritual obstacles including a lack of worthiness, existential questions about the meaning and purpose of life, a negative view of God, and increased insecurity in attachment to God. Also, unresolved religious questions about the beliefs they grew up with, disillusionment about their faith or religious beliefs, distrust, anger, guilt, and other miscellaneous obstacles.[24,25]

Level 4: Adoption of health risk behaviors. In an attempt to manage their social, emotional, psychological and spiritual problems, people adopt behaviors that put their health at risk. According to Dr. Robert Anda, one of the ACE researchers, research accredits 78% of adult IV drug use to unhealed, unaddressed childhood trauma. In addition, research accredits 65% of alcoholism and 50% of general drug abuse to unhealed, unaddressed childhood trauma. A focus on obesity, or food addiction, is how Dr. Felitti started his research on ACEs. In another study of obese and morbidly obese patients, researchers found that 66% identified at least one or more adverse childhood experience, most commonly physical and verbal abuse.[26] The likelihood of having a BMI of 40 or more, the cut-off for morbid obesity, increases significantly as the number of ACE increases.[27]

However, that's not all. Research has been around a long time that proves smoking cigarettes causes cancer, and the government outlawed smoking in most public places. People who smoke pay huge prices and excessive taxes for cigarettes. Fifty years after the Surgeon General's first warning about cancer and smoking, it remains the leading cause of preventable deaths in the United States and kills 443,000 people each year![28] In addition, there is a clear "smoking divide". While smoking rates have declined overall, in poorer populations, the decline is significantly slower. It's especially slow at poorer counties like Kentucky where, in one county, nearly everyone still smokes.[29] According to the ACE study, a male child with an ACE score of six or more is 250% more likely to smoke as an adult. Therefore, it appears that the use of substances, like drugs, alcohol, food and cigarettes, actually is an attempt to deal with a problem. While people know the risk, the immediate reward of the substance might just be worth the later risk of addiction, disease, and death.[30]

Level 5: Disability, diseases and social problems. The adoption of risky behaviors leads to physical and mental disabilities, diseases, and social/family problems. As the number of ACE (0-10) increases, the more likely a person is to experience heart disease, chronic lung disease, stroke, diabetes, cancer, lung cancer, liver disease, injuries, HIV and STDs. While some of these diseases are a result, perhaps, of risky life choices, heart disease is also be linked directly to ACEs due to the chronic stress created by childhood trauma. One study of Native American women in a primary care setting found out that 77% reported childhood physical or sexual abuse or severe neglect.[31] The higher the ACE score, the harder time an individual may have in making a living. There is a graded relationship between ACE scores, Absenteeism, Serious Financial Problems and Job Problems. The more ACEs, the more likelihood of an adult having had 50 or more sexual partners and being at risk of unwanted pregnancy, socially transmitted diseases, and HIV/AIDs. The more adverse experiences one has as a child, the higher the risk of becoming a victim of domestic violence. This is the case for both women and men. Just as the risk of becoming a VICTIM of domestic violence rises with the number of ACEs, so does the risk of perpetrating domestic violence, as applicable to both men and women.

Level 6: Early Death. The peak of the pyramid is early death. A person with an ACE score of 6 or more has a *decreased life expectancy of 20 years*. While the average life expectancy in the United States is climbing toward 80 and even 90, many childhood trauma survivors in the ACE study are dying 20 years earlier.

The studies on childhood trauma that demonstrate the links to adult problems is compelling! Yet most people don't know anything about it. As Christians, we operate under the belief that we are immune, but we aren't. While research does show that people who attend church and believe that God is for them and not against them make less risky choices, research of a church-going population found that the same obstacles to spiritual growth were present when a person experienced childhood trauma.[32] Additionally, we may have adopted survival responses that affect our family directly and pass the trauma down generation after generation. Christians are a part of the world and what affects our neighbor affects us. We are part of the community and we are supposed to be light and salt, a place for hope and healing. Just like flying with a child, we have to put the mask on our self before we can put it on our children.

In addition, we, of course, have bodies. When we experience salvation, it is the rebirth of our spirit, not the rebirth of our body. Our bodies are still impacted by a fallen and broken world, even if we don't want them to be. Our bodies and our choices are not perfect and won't be until heaven. When I eat too many sweets to try to numb my anxiety, it affects my body just as it would anyone else's. I have to live with that impact and God may not heal these consequences until I get a new body in Heaven. Nevertheless, while trauma creates pain, loss, disease, social problems, and early death, *God still heals.* He has wired us for connection, and He has wired us to heal. Connection is something God uses to help us heal. However, this kind of healing doesn't start on the surface, it begins on the inside.

INSIDE-OUT HEALING

One famous scientist said, "Science is thinking God's thoughts after Him."[33] God designed us to heal physically from the inside out; it's wired into our DNA. When my middle daughter, Nikki, was around 9 years old, she was carrying some drinking glasses from upstairs to the dishwasher downstairs. She decided to jump over something and lost her balance. She fell, banging the glasses into each other and they broke. It cut her hand between her thumb and pointer finger. There was a lot of blood and, fortunately, my husband was the first on the scene. Knowing that I don't do well with blood—pass out!—he washed it out and stopped the bleeding before calling me into the room. Using all of my courage, I looked inside the cut. I could see what I thought was the white of a tendon. As calmly as I could, I told her it would probably need stitches. We drove to the emergency room but the doctor said he would not be putting in stitches, however. He said they would use Superglue™, or at least a product that was only one molecule different from the version of Superglue™ we use at home for repairs. He said that the military used this product on the battlefield because it seals the wound preventing bacteria from entering and causing infection. In addition, we wouldn't have to return to get it removed. Since the body heals from the inside-out, as it healed, it would push the Superglue™ "plug" out and eventually it would just pop out of the skin. Sure enough, several weeks later, Nikki came up, "Mommy, the glue popped out of my hand!" It's amazing what learning to work with God's created design for healing can do!

God is consistent, and because He designed physical healing to work this way, emotional healing should work the same way, inside out. God, of course, can heal any way He chooses to because He is above His creation. However, it does seem that He mostly works *with* His creation and follows the physical laws He put in place. Because the outside is visible, we tend to focus on the importance of looking good on the outside. Jesus knew this about people and said that we should pay more attention to the inside first, and then the outside will come into line with the inside. The outside is actually a reflection of the inside, similar to the way a mirror reflects your image back to you (Matthew 23: 25-28).

Our spirit, the part of us that lives on forever, is the core part of us. The part that is born-again when we choose salvation through Christ. When we are born again, this new life moves through the rest of our being starting inside and moving out. Think of it as concentric circles, like a dartboard. Your spirit is instantly made alive through salvation, and then God's renewing power moves outward through the rest of your identity—your mind, will and emotions. Your identity is formed by the interaction of your spirit, your genetics (brain, body, personality), and your mind. Your mind is your conscious awareness, what you think and feel, your memories, your ability to make decisions and choices. Your mind emanates from your brain, and your brain is inside your body. Your behaviors happen outside, but their genesis is inside, beginning with your identity and influenced by your spirit.

This is a complicated concept and many people have tried to conceptualize ways to explain it. One part of you can't be separated from the other until you die. Traumatic experiences wound the innermost part of us, our identity. God seems to have designed us to heal in the same order, from the inside out. We find several clues to this in the scripture. In Matthew 13:1-9 and 18-23, Jesus told a parable about a farmer who went out to plant his seeds. Farmers know that if you want to plant something, you have to clear out what was already there; you have to till the soil and prepare it. In this parable, the farmer was planting by hand rather than by machine, so some of the seeds fell on the pathway next to the garden. The ground was hard and the seeds couldn't even begin to penetrate the soil so they were trampled on, or birds came and ate them. Some of the seeds fell in the shrub next to the garden where there were thorny bushes and weeds. They grew, but so did the thorns and the weeds. Eventually, the growing plants were choked and died.

Some of the seeds fell on what looked, on the surface, like well-tilled soil, but underneath were rocks. When the seeds grew and began to put down their roots, they bumped into the rocks and could only go so far. While the plants began to grow on the surface, they couldn't get enough water or sustenance to maintain the growth and, when the hot sun came out, it burned up the plant and killed what had grown. Some of the seeds however made it into the well-tilled, well-prepared soil of the garden plot. There, the seeds started putting down roots that could grow deep in the soil. On the surface, they formed mature plants that grew and produced a harvest of food. Farmers know that soil perfect for planting doesn't just "happen", it's tilled, prepared, watered, and fed.

Think of the soil as a person's heart or mind. Trauma is like the rocks in the soil; while you might not see them from the surface, they are there and they get in the way of your completing the mandate Paul wrote in Colossians 2: 6-7, "And now, just as you accepted Christ Jesus as your Lord, you must continue to follow him. Let your roots grow down into him, and let your lives be built on him. Then your faith will grow strong in the truth you were taught, and you will overflow with thankfulness." As you put these two thoughts together, you can see that rocks lodged in the "soil" of your mind or your personal identity, keeps your roots from growing down deep into Christ.

Trauma is similar to a bomb buried in your brain. Bombs buried beneath the surface in war-torn countries can stay hidden for a long time. You can't tell it's there until it explodes, destroying the person or animal stepping on it. Traumatic experiences lurk beneath the surface of our minds, hiding from plain sight, until one day something happens that triggers it and, KABOOM!!! It explodes all over you. Fortunately, God knows the location of the bombs in your brain and He knows how to diffuse them.

Imagine holding a Styrofoam cup. This cup represents your in-ner-most self, your personal identity. Now, on the outside write the four basic human needs, Love, Acceptance, Worth, and Security. You can recall these easily by remembering the acronym L. A. W. S. Space them around the cup so that the whole cup is used. All humans are born with these needs and we all long to have our cup filled. We ex-perience disappointment, hurt, anger, and loss when we don't get our needs adequately met. Inside the bottom of the cup, write the word "Fear". We *all* experience fear; fear of not being loved, not being ac-cepted, not feeling worth and not feeling secure. Having our needs met helps us to manage our fear. As a child, God's design for our rela-tionship with our parents is for *them* to meet these basic needs and then, as we mature, we should transfer our dependency for these needs onto God.

Instead, we transfer these needs on to other people and other things. For example, when we get into a relationship, we expect that person will meet these needs for us so we hold our cup out to them and, for a while, it seems to work. Then, they stop filling our cup and we become disappointed, maybe even angry, bitter or resentful. In John 4:1-4 the disciple John tells of a time when Jesus met a Samaritan woman by a well and offered her "living water." She had been married five times and the man she was living with wasn't one of those hus-bands. She kept searching for her needs met through relationships with men, but she continued to be disappointed, disillusioned, and most likely exploited.

While holding the Styrofoam cup, use your pen to poke holes around the bottom half of the cup. This is what the experience of ad-versity or trauma does to your identity; it punches holes in your cup. Therefore, when you point your cup at others, jobs, success, etc., or even at God, it flows out the holes and you are *still* not satisfied. Your fear increases and you become desperate! That is when people turn to sex, drugs, or alcohol to numb the pain. However, when we turn to God, He wants to heal the "holes." He wants to plug them so that when He fills us, we don't continue to feel empty, just like He wanted to heal the Samaritan woman. He wanted her to stop turning to men, and start turning to Him. Do you have holes in your cup? Perhaps holes you haven't even been aware of. Are you ready to let God heal them?

Let God dig the rocks out of your life and prepare the soil of your identity. Let God diffuse the bombs buried in your brain, so that they stop blowing up your life. Let God plug the holes in your cup and daily re-fill you with His perpetual love, acceptance, worth, and security. In the next chapter, I will be introducing Strategic Trauma and Abuse Recovery© which consists of three Strategic Phases of Healing©. These three phases are further broken down into stages in order to provide a map or path to follow as you begin this healing from the inside, out.

Chapter 1 Summary

1. Pain is a problem, but NO pain is not the answer.

2. Psychological or emotional pain is similar to physical pain and demands a response.

3. Because we don't know what to do about it, psychological pain or trauma gets buried beneath shame, guilt, and fear. When it comes to psychological trauma, time does not heal, it conceals.

4. "If it happened when I was a child, it doesn't affect me anymore" is a myth Even if it's been 50 or 60 years since it happened, it's still affecting you in some way.

5. We learn what we live and we live what we learn. Just because you don't repeat the same exact pattern doesn't mean it's not affecting you.

6. The impact of childhood trauma is pervasive and devastating, leading to multiple emotional, social, psychological, physical, spiritual and financial issues. Amongst other things, an ACE score of 6 or more can cause up to a 20-year shortening of your lifespan!

7. The Parable of the Farmer planting seed is a good analogy to explain the impact of trauma in a person's life. The rocks in the soil are like traumatic events in the mind or identity that get in the way of our roots growing down deep into Christ.

8. Your "inside" is your personal identity, and God heals traumatic stress from the inside out. He can dig the rocks out of the soil of your identity and diffuse the bombs buried there that keep blowing up your life. He can plug the holes in your cup.

9. Strategic Trauma and Abuse Recovery© or S.T.A.R. provides a map for walking through the process of healing from trauma and will be introduced in the next chapter.

CHAPTER 2:
IT'S NOT YOUR FAULT,
BUT IT IS YOUR PROBLEM

"God uses men who are weak and feeble enough to lean on him."

J. Hudson Taylor

WRONG PLACE, WRONG TIME

In 1988, I was walking across a quiet street alone, around 10:00 p.m. I noticed a couple walking along, carrying groceries, talking and laughing. A quiet voice inside of me said, "Get in your car and lock the doors!" However, I took my time, put some things in my hatchback, and then went around unlocking the door. I had just taken the key out of the lock when I heard someone running up behind me. He grabbed me by the throat, threatened me with a knife in my back and shoved me down inside of my car. I had turned to face him and pulled my knees up to my chest hoping to kick him and keep him off me. I was screaming and yelling; I was terrified!

Just as no one grows up with the desire or plan to become an alcoholic, no one grows up with a desire or plan to become a trauma victim. I certainly didn't! "How did I get here?" is a question we all ask ourselves. Following the assault, I decided to attend a rape prevention class conducted through a local adult learning center. While I hadn't been raped and was able to escape, my belief was that because it happened at all, I must have done something wrong and needed to learn how to prevent this from happening again. The teacher was a veteran police detective with a unique teaching style. He sat behind a desk, leaning back in his chair with his feet propped up on it. As a fellow event speaker, I was appalled at the way he rambled for a while and then finally allowed for questions. I raised my hand and shared with the audience what had happened to me. They all gasped appreciatively. Then I asked him my question, "What did I do wrong?" He peered at me from behind his feet and said with a Texas drawl, "Well, are you alive?" "Obviously," I retorted. "Then you didn't do anything wrong. You were just in the wrong place at the wrong time, and you were available." Those simple words were helpful to me. While they didn't keep me from being terrified, hesitant, reliving the experience, panicking, locking myself in my apartment, basically all the "post-rape syndrome" symptoms that people have, it did help me to stop blaming myself for the event occurring.

Many years later, I found myself extremely angry. I couldn't understand why I was SO angry all the time. I had a good life. I married a wonderful man; we had three children, and I developed a trauma ministry in my church. I was looking at myself in the mirror one day and asked God, "What is wrong with me?" I heard His still small voice in my heart, "You know that trauma thing you write and teach and counsel people about? You have it! That's why you are angry and it's time to deal with it." "Of course!" I thought. While I had been to therapy with a great therapist following the assault and following the abusive relationship that had me at the location of the assault in the first place, my counselor had not addressed it as *trauma*. She had inadvertently, reinforced my idea that somehow all of this was my fault. Her type of counseling left me believing that the perpetration was all about me and that I had somehow caused it because of my choices. She did not reinforce the other message of the police detective, that I was *in the wrong place at the wrong time* and that a perpetrator had set his sight on me. Therefore, the influence of the trauma remained in my brain, including the anger, and I had never fully healed.

Similarly, one of the researchers of The ACE Study says, "Expressions like 'self-destructive behavior' are misleading and should be dropped because, while describing the acceptance of long-term risk, they overlook the importance of the obvious short-term benefits."[34] Blaming the victim doesn't help, and doesn't work. It only makes things worse. Blaming yourself doesn't help, and it doesn't work. It only increases your shame and sense of helplessness. If you had actual power to prevent it, you certainly would have used that power. However, even though it isn't your fault, it is your problem. You have to take responsibility for where you are NOW, even if you don't know how you got here. One of the questions I continued to ask myself was, "What's wrong with me?" What God pointed me to was, "What's happened to me?" Changing the focus of this question allows me to move from defeat to empowerment.

Wherever you are right now, whether you've made the journey up the ACE pyramid or not, let's talk about how you got to where you are right now. Understanding your journey will help you understand how to heal.

THE SIX STAGES OF BUILDING A TRAUMA SURVIVOR: THE TRAUMA SURVIVOR BLUEPRINT©[35]

Human beings are complex and sometimes difficult to understand. Hundreds, even thousands of theories exist to explain human motivation and behavior. As mentioned in the previous chapter, our personal identity is a constant interaction between our brain—genetically pre-programed with certain expectations and needs—and our experiences which shape our expectations, values and beliefs.

To explain how a person goes from a non-affected, non-trauma survivor to developing a Trauma Survivor Identity, I've put together what I call The Trauma Survivor Blueprint©.

First, an event outside of your conscious control occurs and contradicts your expectations, beliefs, values, and/or needs (personal identity), and you immediately experience loss. Second, your brain interprets the contradictions as threatening and triggers the Limbic System of your brain. The Limbic System is a convenient way of referring to several interrelated structures in the brain, which are involved in motivation, emotion, learning and memory.[36] You might think of it as the "fight, flight, fright or freeze" part of the brain. God designed it to take action when you are threatened. Third, because you experienced loss when the contradictions occurred, it starts the grief response. If the loss is resolved, the grief stops here. If this loss can't be resolved, the loss remains active along with the accompanying emotions and, the grief (and healing) process is stuck.

For example, let's say that you are a teenager and you are at home. You hear your parents arguing. They yell at each other and call each other names. They've never done this before! Your mom throws something at your dad. He calls her a bitch and runs at her, grabs her and starts choking her. They are screaming and yelling and someone calls the police.

Obviously, an event like this would contradict your expectations and beliefs about how your parents are supposed to behave. Your need for security and safety would be compromised. You would feel terrified, worried, and panicked, maybe even embarrassed and sad. You would also lose some respect for your parents, your view of a healthy marriage, your desire to be around them, and your sense of safety and security. If your parents resolve this by apologizing and forgiving each other, then apologizing to you it can be resolved, if you chose to forgive them. Your grief would stop here and you wouldn't become a trauma survivor. However, if they don't resolve it with you, you must adjust and the next phase in your development of a Trauma Survivor begins.

Fourth, your brain rallies to survive and you will put into action new survival behaviors, thoughts, and attitudes. This includes external behaviors and internal behaviors like trying to forget about it or pretending it never happened. Survival responses almost work to manage your pain. In fact, they may work quite well, temporarily. If something like this happens again, you might jump in the middle and try to stop it. You might start spending more time away from home with other people. You may even start yelling and screaming or attacking people like your parents are doing. Fifth, your brain automatically evaluates your own responses. Sixth, if these responses also contradict your own expectations of yourself, it triggers your Limbic System again and you experience additional loss and additional grief emotion, which remains active in the brain.

Ongoing, unresolved trauma is the result when you keep cycling through this loop, developing more survival responses (behaviors, thoughts, attitudes) on top of previous survival responses. You are now developing new survival responses because of the original event, but also survival responses to your own survival responses. This process moves you further and further away from a conscious awareness of the starting point: the original painful event.

The results of this continuous cycling are that your perception of your very "self" changes, your perception of your personal identity changes, and you adopt a "survivor" identity. Thinking about the ACE pyramid, people move from traumatic experiences to embrace risky behaviors, which serve as survival responses. Looking back, they now perceive these responses as unrelated to the trauma, "this is just who I am," they think. Moving on up the pyramid, these choices create, or at least contribute to disease, disability and social problems. Friends, family, and society in general see these problems as bad choices and bad behavior resulting from their poor character. For many people, not all, these ongoing issues lead to early death—all while "forgetting" the genesis or beginning of where this whole thing started—a misdirected attempt to survive the wound of trauma. Because the conscious link between your current survival responses and the original wound are not in your conscious awareness, you are unable to address it directly. This can happen no matter who you are. It's not a matter of how smart you are or what kind of character you have. It's because you have a brain. Wherever you go, you take your brain with you.

Of course, the Blueprint does not explain ALL bad behavior. People sin and make mistakes. No one is perfect. However, many Christians feel trapped in negative patterns or in patterns of sin because their brain has become convinced that the immediate relief of the substance or repetitive behavior outweighs the long-term risk. While it does temporarily provide relief from the pain of the wound, it doesn't actually heal the wound.

Of the six stages in the Trauma Survivor Blueprint, the survival responses are the only stage visible to both the survivor and others around them. Behavior has obvious and sometimes immediate and visible consequences for the survivor and for people around them. People can't see inside to a person's thoughts or painful memories, but they can feel their anger, withdrawal, or intense sadness. Therefore, you and those around you begin to judge you based on your survival responses. You begin to believe you ARE your survival responses, and other people begin to believe that too. You define your identity by your survival responses, and not who God created you to be, or whom the Bible says you are in-Christ.

I grew up moving frequently because my father was good at his job and kept getting promotions. This pattern fit my parents own survival responses of moving due to their childhood trauma. Making friends and then moving away was very hard on me. When I would arrive at a new school, children were cruel and would exclude me at first, even bully me. I survived by learning to spend time alone, and would eventually make friends. My dad encouraged to remain distant, knowing we would be moving. My teachers and other students came to see me as aloof, independent, and even stuck-up. Eventually, I began to believe I didn't fit in anywhere.

As an adult, I continued to feel like an outsider. I met and married a good Christian man and, even though my husband and I lived in the same general area and attended the same church for 13+ years, I still felt like an outsider. God began to show me that I frequently dismissed people, especially other women. This was a habit because my brain was still operating under the assumption that "there was no point in getting to know them since they wouldn't like me anyway since I am an outsider and I'd be leaving soon." This even contributes, I know now, to why I have such difficulty remembering people's names.

While this type of behavior might have worked to protect me from feeling ridiculed and embarrassed or from hurt when I had to move again as a child or teenager, now as an adult, these survival behaviors have gotten in the way of my forming friendships with other women. I wasn't beaten or abused so it didn't seem like there could be a trauma issue here. However, I learned to see the world through a lens of "I don't belong". Therefore, that's how I approached all parts of my life.

Can you see how even nonviolent traumatic experiences might have shaped the lens of your life and influenced negatively the way you approach relationships?

THE THREE PHASES OF STRATEGIC TRAUMA AND ABUSE RECOVERY[©]

It is widely accepted in the field of psychology that successful trauma recovery occurs in three general phases, safety, grieving, and reconnecting.[37] I've personalized them some and titled the phases as follows: Phase 1-Establishing Safety and Stabilization, Phase 2-Reprocessing and Grieving, Phase 3- Reconnecting and Integrating.

The beginning and ending of recovery are not cut-and-dry, just as moving from one phase to the next is not like walking from one room into another. Think of it as an "open-concept" house; you may be in the kitchen, but you can see into the living room and dining room. When do you leave the kitchen and arrive in the dining room? You probably won't cross a line which defines the boundary. However, when you are sitting at the table eating, you know for sure you are in the dining room. Research has shown that people move through these phases as they recover. Phase 2: Reprocessing and Grieving, is the "heart" of the process. Phase 1 is preparing for the heart of the process by establishing a modicum of internal safety and external stabilization, and Phase 3 is integrating and reconnecting with your life and relationships after completing the grief process. Healing isn't completed just because the formal grieving work is done. You will still have to change some habits, hang-ups, and other issues more directly.

Because these phases are still very broad, however, I've broken them down further into individual stages to make them more understandable and maneuverable. These are:

Phase One—Safety and Stabilization: Characterized by Feeding Your FAITH in God

1. I admit that I am wounded and I am accepting that I am powerless over the wound, the wounding, and the one creating the wound.

2. I have decided to give up trying to fix myself and I will humbly seek healing from God (or you can say my Higher Power), while fully understanding that healing will require my participation.

3. I am accepting that I have to grieve in order to heal and I'm determined to allow myself to feel as I move through the healing process even though it will be painful and scary at times.

4. I am forming a partnership with at least one other person (counselor or recovery coach) with whom I will move on to Phase Two in order to boldly identify (and finish grieving the sources of) my wounds in a focused and structured manner.

Phase Two—Reprocessing and Grieving: Characterized by Snowballing Your HOPE in God

1. I am courageously choosing to tell my story using structure and detail to my counselor/recovery coach, and, when possible, my fellow group members.

2. I am identifying the beliefs that have grown out of the hurtful events; beliefs about me, life, others, and God (spirituality, religion, or church) along with my initial responses.

3. I am humbly identifying and admitting to myself and my partner or group, my own survival responses even when they contradict my own expectations of myself.

4. I am embracing and grieving all of the losses I experienced with this source of trauma; those the offender caused me, and those caused by my own survival responses.

5. After completing this thorough inventory of my experiences, contradicted expectations, losses, survival behaviors and the losses these caused me, I humbly and courageously choose for-

giveness; forgiving my perpetrator for robbing me and forgiving myself (as I have been forgiven) for my responses.

6. I understand that healing is an ongoing process from the inside, out, and I humbly acknowledge where I've come from and those who have contributed to my healing and will make a spiritual marker to represent where God has met me on my path of healing from this source of trauma.

PHASE THREE--RECONNECTING AND INTEGRATING: CHARACTERIZED BY ACTIVATING YOUR LOVE FOR GOD AND OTHERS.

1. I am remaining open to identifying other wounds in my life that need to be healed, without attempting to heal them myself, while maintaining a willing attitude to work through these steps again if necessary, or to assist someone else who needs to work through these steps to healing.

2. I am intentionally beginning to move toward reconnecting with myself, with God, and with others.

Each phase focuses on a specific characteristic of spiritual development. In 1 Corinthians 13:13 Paul wrote, "Three things will last forever—faith, hope, and love—and the greatest of these is love." You may have spent a lot of energy and time trying to be more loving, only to find you failed. Love is a behavior, not a feeling. It's on the outside and a reflection of the inside. First, we need start with the inside where you store your faith. Feeding our faith leads to hope. Snowballing or building up our hope leads naturally to expressing love.

These stages help to focus your attention on the inside, allowing the wound of trauma to heal naturally. You will read and learn about each stage, working through them and moving you through the healing process. You will probably take more than a day or week to work through each stage. This isn't a "12-day plan for total transformation." This is a long-term healing process completed by God in partnership with us.

UNDERSTANDING PHASE ONE:
ESTABLISHING SAFETY AND STABILIZATION

Trauma, childhood or adult onset, leads to a continuous or periodic state of feeling unsafe or unstable. In the previous chapter, I presented some of the outcomes of the Adverse Childhood Experiences study. The Limbic System is the part of the brain switched on and it remains on if the trauma wound isn't healed intentionally. When you feel unsafe, you make choices to do things that help you to feel safer. These survival responses tend to fall into the four categories of fight, flee, freeze, and fix.

When you are a fighter, you might fight with everyone. You are angry and resistant, you walk around with a chip on your shoulder, you might attack people unprovoked, and you might always defend yourself. If you are one who flees, you are running away from problems and difficult situations. People run away in different ways, maybe actually leave, abandon a relationship, and stay too busy to think about things, or distract themselves from the real painful traumatic memories. If you freeze, you might stay emotionally cold, distant, stuck, trying not to move and maybe you are subconsciously trying to be invisible. I think of the freeze response as a rabbit sitting completely still in a field, hoping predators won't see it. Fixing can look like fixing one's self or others—always trying to fix yourself with self-help books, fads, etc.

Most of us do each of these at some time or another. There is nothing wrong with them in and of themselves. Survival is important, and it's wired into us by God to want to survive. Most of the time, these are automatic responses, like a reflex. We may not be aware we are even doing it. Most psychologists call these "symptoms". Rather than calling these "symptoms", I prefer the term "survival choices" or "survival responses". These choices are not out of a "fear of success", nor have you chosen "self-defeating behaviors". They are actual attempts to survive. Unfortunately, the side effects of some responses can be disastrous. Fighting ruins relationships and leaves you lonely. Fleeing ruins relationships, wears you out, and leaves you alone. Freezing keeps you safe, but stuck, and once again, alone. Fixing is exhausting! While you might not be alone, you may end up feeling lonely, drained and defeated, since the "fixes" are only temporary.

You may be in so much pain that you are willing to put your faith in the substance in front of you, the relationship being offered, the temporary fix, or your own strength and power, because it does work—at least for now. You might ignore the long-term consequences, because a long-term solution doesn't seem possible or probable. While you might not be aware you are even doing these things to survive, as God brings it to your awareness, you can consider the choice to choose the fifth "F" of survival, which is faith.

FAITH: FINDING SAFETY IN CHRIST

The antidote to feeling unsafe and unstable is faith in God. While many people think of faith as religion, I'm defining faith to mean the firm or confident belief in something that has not yet been proved. While there might be evidence that healing is possible, it hasn't yet happened. Faith is not the opposite of doubt, but the opposite of certainty. Without faith, a person can't move through the Safety and Stabilization Phase. Without faith, a person isn't able to move into the Reprocessing and Grieving Phase because it's too scary and painful. Fear will overcome you. Faith overcomes fear, doubt, anxiety, and worry. Without faith, hope will wither.

The 11th chapter of Hebrews is the "faith" chapter because the writer lists very important ancestors of the Hebrew people who made choices based on faith in God. However, if you read the entire Old Testament, you will see that many other people made decisions based on faith in something else. People invest their faith in many different things. This includes your own strength, your own power of influence and change. We put faith in other people, like our spouse or child. We put faith in our jobs, our pastor, and our friends. All of these things are good things in which to invest some faith. However, what happens when you have money invested and the investment doesn't pan out or goes bankrupt? You lose your investment! The more you have invested in yourself, the more you lose when you do something disappointing, and additionally, the more pressure you feel to be perfect.

Faith in any amount can grow or shrink. Just like a savings account, the interest can compound and increase; or if you spend it without replacing it, the amount will shrink. Jesus used another parable about faith using yeast placed in flour to make bread dough. "The Kingdom of Heaven is like the yeast a woman used in making bread. Even though she put only a little yeast in three measures of flour, it permeated every part of the dough." (Matthew 13:33) A small amount of yeast goes a long way when it's fed. Bakers know that yeast has to be alive and they have to feed it. When yeast remains packaged up and not used, it dies. When fed with warm water and even a little sugar, it grows, expands, and gives off a gas that causes bread to rise. No matter how much faith you have in God, you can feed it and it will grow. If you starve it, it will shrink.

In another parable, Jesus said, "If you had faith even as small as a mustard seed, you could say to this mulberry tree, 'May you be uprooted and thrown into the sea,' and it would obey you!" (Luke 17:6) Mustard seeds are about 1-2 mm in diameter—very small. Nevertheless, when you plant, water, and feed them, they grow into huge bushy trees, big enough for birds and other animals to nest in or to eat. In fact, once mustard is planted, it's difficult to get rid of! When your faith is firmly planted, watered, and fed, it too will be difficult to get rid of.

FEED YOUR FAITH

There are different activities that feed our faith. These might include thinking about God, learning about God, reading about God, or talking about God. However, if that is as far as we go, how much have we actually invested our faith in God? Think of a famous person, like Harrison Ford, for example. Most people in America know he is a famous actor. Let's say you get on his Facebook page and read all about him, follow him on Twitter, read books about him, visit the IMDB website to look at his pictures, study his career and can tell anyone anything that they want to know about him. Then one day you are at the grocery store and who should be there but Harrison Ford! If you run up to him, hug him, and talk to him like a long-lost friend, telling him everything you know about him, what might his response be? He may be friendly, but then again he may have you arrested as a stalker! Knowing about Harrison Ford is not the same as knowing Harrison Ford. Stalking is not the same as knowing.

To know someone you have to spend time communicating with them, which involves talking to them and listening to them. You also have to open up, be honest, be vulnerable and they have to reciprocate. It's only through this ongoing sharing from heart-to-heart that relationships really are truly formed. Shame, fear, a sense of being unsafe, and anxiety all get in the way of your doing this with anyone, including God. In fact, many times you aren't even aware of guarding yourself against getting hurt.

Many of us have learned to stalk God, but not to really connect with Him. Many of us are afraid to connect to Him. One place to begin feeding your faith in God is by talking to Him and listening to Him. When you are attracted to someone, you approach him or her and find a way to strike up a conversation. You can do the same thing with God. When we have a conversation with God, it's called "prayer". Just as you would with a person, it's best to start simply.

SIMPLE PRAYER

Billy Graham says, "Prayer is simply a two-way conversation between you and God. It is not the body's posture but the heart's attitude that counts when we pray."[38] According to theologian Richard Foster, "Simple Prayer involves ordinary people bringing ordinary concerns to a loving and compassionate Father. There is no pretense in Simple Prayer. We do not pretend to be more holy, more pure, or more saintly than we actually are. We do not try to conceal our conflicting and contradictory motives from God—or ourselves. And in this posture, we pour out our heart to the God who is greater than our heart and who knows all things (1 John 3:20)."[39]

Looking back at what we call The Lord's Prayer, Jesus said we should ask simply for what we need. We should feel perfectly free to complain to God, to laugh with God at a joke, to ask Him a question, to cry, even to yell at God. In Jeremiah 20:7-8, Jeremiah complains to God about being a household joke. Jeremiah may have even said this prayer with his fist raised and shaking it at God!

Simple prayer is the most common prayer in the Bible. Some examples include Moses - Numbers 11:11b-12; Elisha - 2 Kings 2:23-24; and David - Psalm 137:9. These same people also recorded awe-inspiring prayers: Moses - Exodus 32:32; Elisha - 2 Kings 4:13; and David - Psalm 119:97.

There are some common misunderstandings about prayer identified by theologian Richard Foster in his book, *Prayer - 10th Anniversary Edition: Finding the Heart's True Home.* Perhaps one or more of these misunderstandings is keeping you from praying or from praying more.

1. We have to get our lives right before God hears us pray. God hears us when we pray. God saves us by His grace, we live by His grace, and we pray by His grace. Of course, praying to Him takes faith; repeating prayers just to say them without directing them *to* Him and at least hoping He hears them is like reading a poem with no one in the room. It's a great exercise, but you are just speaking to hear yourself speak. No one who spoke to Jesus had their lives together; yet when they asked to be healed, He healed them—ALL of them that asked, and some who didn't even ask out loud.

2. We have to "master" prayer as we master playing the piano or gymnastics. All of us come to God with all kinds of motives and God Himself is big enough to unravel all of our mixed motives. Jesus says, just talk to God as if we are talking to a parent asking for something. (Matthew 7:7-9)

3. We might get it wrong! To God, there are no bad prayers. He doesn't really care about grammar, your posture, where you are or what direction you are facing at the moment. God accepts us just as we are and hears our prayers just as they are. He listens to our hearts as well as our words. You can't get it wrong!

Therefore, while it is a good practice to pray aloud some of the time, you can carry on an ongoing conversation with God in your head. Here are some tips on learning how to pray suggested by Richard

Foster.[40] You can use these if you are a beginner, or if you are more experienced, to encourage you in your recovery from trauma.

TIPS FOR SIMPLE PRAYER

1. Keep it simple. Prayer is nothing more than an ongoing and growing love relationship with God the Father, Son, and Holy Spirit. It's just like talking to another loved one like a spouse, a girlfriend or boyfriend, or your child. It's a way of starting and continuing a connection.

2. Never be discouraged by your lack of prayer. If you notice a lack, that means you have a desire. Pray that God will grow the desire. Remember, a mustard seed size or a yeast grain size of faith is all you need to get started. You just have to water it and feed it.

3. Don't try too hard to pray. Occasional joggers don't suddenly run a marathon. It takes practice. Start with praying for just a few seconds or a few minutes. Don't try to pray for 3 hours! Just pray simple thoughts and desires.

4. Pray even when you are sinning. Even when you are angry or face temptation, talk to God about it. Something like, "God I know I really shouldn't be doing this right now! I don't want to be so angry. Help me please!" There are plenty of examples in the Bible about others praying during these times.

In simple prayer, we are the subject. But, if you keep this practice up, you will change your brain from turning toward self, or food, or drugs, or alcohol, or a person or whatever else you are putting more faith in, and turn toward God more than you are now. As Foster writes, "We pass from thinking of God as part of our life to the realization that we are part of his life."[41]

SAMPLE SIMPLE PRAYERS FOR HEALING FROM THE HIDDEN WOUNDS OF TRAUMA

Here is a sample of simple prayer: "Dear Jesus, I really need to learn how to pray more. But, if I am really honest, a lot of times I don't even want to pray. Help me to want to pray more and forget to pray less. In your name, Amen."

If you aren't experienced in asking God for anything, or even if you are, here are some suggested prayers regarding healing to get you started:

Okay God, if you are there, I'm going to try to talk to you. I guess what I need is some hope that you might really be listening. But I'm going to practice believing that you are hearing me and that maybe you might care. Bye for now.

God, I want to believe that you can heal me from all this pain. Please show me something that gives me hope this week. Amen.

Jesus, you said that the weary and weak should come to you and you will give them rest. Well I'm exhausted and I'm so weak. Please tell me what to do to feel better. Amen.

Okay God, so I'm going to begin this healing process stuff that this lady says might help me but I'm really not sure. I really don't think it will do anything for me, but I want to believe that it will. I want to believe that you can really change my life. Please help me to believe more that my future will be better than my past. In the name of Jesus, amen.

Dear God, Please help me to accept that I've been wounded and understand what "powerless" looks like, because I really don't know! Amen.

MAKING A PRAYER COMMITMENT

Each week you are working through this study, it is important to make a prayer commitment. The Prayer Commitment is to acknowledge that this class is not about "changing" you or about you changing yourself. The focus is on healing from the wound of trauma, from the inside, out. Perhaps you have tried changing your thoughts or your trauma-based habits before. This book is about healing and acknowledging that God is the source of all healing, whether it is miraculous or mundane, simple or stupendous. Each week, write out a simple prayer. If you aren't ready to pray, will you think about it? Think about what is keeping you from being ready to pray. It's okay if you aren't ready to pray. God, and these stages of recovery, will meet you where you are.

CHAPTER 2 SUMMARY

1. No one grows up with the desire or plan to be a trauma survivor.

2. Blaming yourself for the experience of trauma doesn't help and it isn't true. You were in the wrong place at the wrong time and were targeted because you were available.

3. While it isn't your fault, it is your problem to deal with!

4. There are six stages of building a trauma survivor. Unfortunately, only one of them is visible, the fourth stage—survival behaviors.

5. Ongoing, unresolved trauma results because you keep cycling through the loop, developing survival responses on top of survival responses, thus moving you further and further away from your God-given identity.

6. While the Trauma Survivor Blueprint© doesn't explain all bad behaviors, many people are trapped in negative patterns of behavior which started as or grew out of survival-based behaviors.

7. The healing process takes place in three phases: Establishing Safety and Stabilization, Reprocessing and Grieving, and Reconnecting and Loving.

8. Each phase focuses on a specific characteristic of spiritual development: Phase One focuses on feeding your faith; Phase Two focuses on snowballing your hope; and Phase Three focuses on activating your love.

9. You invest your faith in lots of different things, and that faith investment can grow or shrink.

10. Feeding your faith in God will grow your faith in God. Faith

involves more than believing that God exists. Investing your faith in God involves having an intimate relationship with Him.

11. You can start feeding your faith in God through simple prayer. To start, make a daily or weekly prayer commitment regarding your emotional healing.

13. A prayer of commitment keeps the focus off you doing the changing, and keeps the focus on asking God for healing.

CHAPTER 3:
EMBRACE
YOUR WEAKNESS

"Your biggest weakness is God's greatest opportunity."

Charles Stanley

Annabelle was in a neighborhood of mobile homes and saw two puppies tied up under one of the homes. They were filthy, skinny, and hot. She wanted to rescue the dogs but the owner wouldn't let them go. She brought some dog food to the owner, but wasn't sure they were being fed properly. The owner never took them inside, never played with them, and never cuddled with them. She already had four dogs of her own and couldn't imagine taking two more, even if she could convince the owner to let them go. After several weeks, she saved up her own money and offered to purchase the dogs. The owner finally consented and Annabelle approached the puppies. They barked threateningly, defending their space under the mobile home. They saw her as an intruder! They didn't know she was there to rescue them. Eventually, after much coaxing, she drove off with the terrified pups.

One puppy was a small breed and she and her husband agreed to keep her with their other rescued dogs. The other, however, was a male and going to be large and possibly part Pit-Bull. There was no way she could keep him! Dog rescue organizations in her area wouldn't take in Pit-Bulls, though. She found a transport going to another state that specialized in placing Pit Bulls, but they were full. She prayed that God would help her find a home for this young male puppy. The day the transport was supposed to leave, the driver called and said they had room for one more dog and if she could get him to them, they would take him. She very quickly loaded him up and took him to the transport. He terrified and shaking. He thought that he was safe where he was originally, chained under the mobile home, exposed to the elements, and without much food or water. He thought that this moving business was the most terrifying thing he had ever experienced in his life. He rode in the crate terrified. He didn't know that at the other end of this ride, he would be placed with a loving family who would feed him, play with him, and cuddle him. This was the most important ride of his life and, if he had just relaxed, he might have enjoyed it. He was powerless and helpless to change his situation, though he continued to try.

I can identify with this puppy; uprooted, moved around, and not really knowing where I am going, and scared to death! Even when I was living in the pain of my wounds, at least it was familiar. The uprooting from my familiar spot felt very unsafe. Like the puppy, God was moving me to a much better, safer place where I could live a more abundant life that I couldn't even imagine at the time. Living in the pain of your wounds from trauma may be familiar to you too, and you may interpret that as safe because that's all you've ever known. Nevertheless, God wants to use this program as a way of uprooting you from that spot and rescuing you from an unsafe place to take you to a place of more abundant life.

THE RUSHING RIVER OF TRAUMA

Lisa TerKeurst, author of "The Best Yes: Making Wise Decisions in the Midst of Endless Demands,"[42] suggests thinking about a decision as a river. If you are standing on the bank watching the water rush by, you have the opportunity to go a different direction. Once you jump in the river, however, the rushing water will take you wherever it happens to be going. I love this analogy. I have tried to adopt this thought process in my life. Unlike self-directed decisions, however, traumatic experiences don't consider our wants, but launch us into the river against our will. We find ourselves thrown in, flailing around and trying to get back to the bank and back to safety. We didn't chose this river, it seems to have chosen us. Now, our only decision seems to be how to navigate the river we've been thrown into. How to navigate to safety while keeping our head above water and not drown.

When I was in my early 20's, I took a group of middle-school-age girls on a rafting trip down the Nantahala River in North Carolina. Most of the eight-mile trip is cold, splashy water, considered class two and three rapids, until you get to the end. There you encounter Nantahala Falls. It's a little scary because if you get stuck on the rocks, the force of the water can tip over your raft and dump you in the 45 degree, fast moving, downhill flow which contains a whirlpool. People dumped out of their rafts can be stuck in the whirlpool and pulled to the bottom where they can drown. Spectators post themselves around to watch this last run down the falls, and outfitters have cameras posted to take pictures of screaming rafters traversing the scariest part of the river. There are also lifeguards ready to help those people who are tossed. However, the guides warn you that they can't come down into the whirlpool to get you. You have to get out of the whirlpool yourself, and then they can help you out of the river. The best advice to get out of a whirlpool is to *relax*. That's right. Hold your breath, relax, stop fighting it, and let the whirlpool run its course and pop you back up to the top, eventually. That behavior is totally against your survival intuition! You want to fight and swim, and claw your way to the top of the water. Unfortunately, that only makes things worse and can cause you to drown.

As the girls and I approached this unnerving waterfall, keeping this in mind, I was scared, but I felt safe. The reason? We had a guide in our raft who had made the run with other novices many times and hadn't lost a single person. After we were on dry ground, we were all relieved and felt safe again. We also felt energized and powerful since we had overcome, as a team, the most difficult rapid on the Nantahala River run.

I think there is a lot to learn about trauma recovery from river rafting on the Nantahala. Having a guide made the journey safer than doing it alone. When we all worked together as a team, we went the direction we planned to go and made the turns we needed to make. While there was still anxiety and fear, we overcame it enough to make it to our destination. We planned for known problems, and worked through them together. We accepted that we were powerless against the river; it was taking us where it was going and fighting against it didn't make sense and could even jeopardize our health. We prepared for the whirlpool. We each reminded ourselves that, if we ended up in it, we had to let go. Just like with the wound of trauma, we would have to accept our powerlessness over the whirlpool and allow it to push us to the surface.

I went a few more times down that stretch of river while still in my 20s with different groups of people. The last time was with a group of adults, most of whom were 20-30 years older than I was. On this particular trip, we opted for a non-guided tour. They elected me to be the raft captain and steer the raft from the back. I had to tell the other five or six people in the raft which way to paddle and turn. I was extremely nervous, especially about the final waterfall. There was one man, a church member and friend, who just could not bring himself to follow my directions. His wife kept fussing at him to do what I said, but he would question it, hesitate, and then do the opposite. This would hang us up on the rocks more often than not.

As we approached the final waterfall, the whole crew told him to follow Denice's directions. However, he just couldn't and we got hung up on the rocks at the top of the waterfall. The rushing water trapped us with such force, that it seemed we would tip over and all end up in the whirlpool at the bottom of the waterfall! To make matters worse, there were other rafts behind us also trying to navigate Nantahala Falls. We blocked one and knocked another across the opening to the falls, putting them off course. Using our paddles against the rocks for leverage, we eventually made it over the boulders and into the falls, though if I remember right, we went down backwards. It wasn't pretty, and we had a few minutes of terror, but we made it safely to shore, soaked and a little embarrassed.

My friend just couldn't trust that I had experience with the river and knew what I was doing. He saw himself as the most capable, even though he wasn't. He didn't know what he was doing. Because of that, he put us all in danger. That was not his intent, of course. He intended to protect himself and the rest of us. If he had let go of his pride and fear enough to let me lead, we would have had a much more pleasant trip. When you are in the rapids of a river, some of the movements are counter-intuitive. Logically, his responses made sense to him. However, my experience on the river had taught me the moves that actually worked. In the end, we were all safe and had a great time. Fortunately, no one was hurt and we had a shared adventure to talk about for a long time.

Similarly, if someone has thrown you into the river of trauma, behavior that seems logical for your survival may not be the best way to navigate your way back on track. To heal from trauma, you too can choose to trust someone to lead you who has experienced navigating the river of trauma recovery.

STAGE 1: REALITY VS. PERCEPTION

The first stage of recovery is a reflection of the reality you find yourself in:

Stage 1: I admit that I am wounded and I am accepting that I am powerless over the wound, the wounding, and the one creating the wound.

Many people confuse reality and perception. Is my perception reality or is there a more concrete reality? The more my perception overlaps with reality, the saner I am. In our world, when a person's perception of himself is extremely different from reality, we consider him to have a mental illness. For example, if the person thinks he is the King of England when actually he is Joe Smith from Paducah, we know he has a problem with reality. This is an extreme example, however all of us live in some type of disconnect from reality. We may call these less obvious disconnections, "blind spots."

According to the Bible, there is an ultimate reality. The more our perception lines up with that reality, the saner we become. Jesus used a parable to talk about this as recorded in Matthew 6:22-23, "Your eye is a lamp that provides light for your body. When your eye is good, your whole body is filled with light. But when your eye is bad, your whole body is filled with darkness. And if the light you think you have is actually darkness, how deep that darkness is! What he is saying is, we *can* be deceived by our own perception of life and reality.

Paul says this in another way in 2 Corinthians 10:4-5, "We use God's mighty weapons, not worldly weapons, to knock down the strongholds of human reasoning and to destroy false arguments. We destroy every proud obstacle that keeps people from knowing God. We capture their rebellious thoughts and teach them to obey Christ." God has a reality and our perception frequently contradicts this reality. Paul is saying here that the number one priority in life is to know God. In order to know God, we have to know Christ because He is the representation of and the bridge to God. Our misperceptions keep us from trusting and obeying Christ, therefore keeping us from knowing and trusting God. Trauma creates and feeds these misperceptions about God as well as misperceptions about others and ourselves.

Perhaps you grew up being told you would never amount to anything, or your perception of your parent's behavior was that you weren't special or loved. On the other hand, perhaps your parents taught you that you are valuable, worthwhile, and worthy of God's love, only to have all of those beliefs contradicted when your Christian spouse cheated on you and abandoned you. As you leave these adverse experiences behind you, your brain goes with you. You don't get a new brain just because you leave the adversity or trauma behind. Your brain has recorded the experiences, its interpretation of those experiences, the contradictions to expectations, the losses, and the emotion you experienced because of the losses. The "files" with all of this information aren't erased or sent to the "trash". Because they are survival-based, you file them away, and compartmentalize them to try to keep your thoughts off them. Unfortunately, whether you like it or not, they continue to run in the background, continue to influence your decisions, your moods, and your interpretations of yourself, others, and God.

THE REALITY OF VULNERABILITY AND WEAKNESS

Facing the reality of trauma means making yourself emotionally vulnerable, something the traumatic experience taught you not to do again. Remarkably, emotional vulnerability is the most accurate measurement of courage.[43] In other words, the more emotionally vulnerable you are willing to make yourself, the more courage you possess. The reality is we are all more vulnerable than we think. You may think you have built up an impenetrable wall of steal around your emotions, around your mind, and around your identity, but it's a false perception. Admitting you are vulnerable is courageous, and recognizing your vulnerability—your true state of being—is recognizing your weakness and an important step in accepting powerlessness. This is lining up your perception with reality.

Isaiah wrote in chapter 40, versus 6-7: A voice says, Cry [prophesy]! And I said, What shall I cry? [The voice answered, Proclaim:] All flesh is as frail as grass, and all that makes it attractive [its kindness, its goodwill, its mercy from God, its glory and comeliness, however good] is transitory, like the flower of the field. The grass withers, the flower fades, when the breath of the Lord blows upon it; surely [all] the people are like grass.[44]

In this recording of Isaiah's prophecies, God told Isaiah to remind the people of their vulnerability, their frailness, their weakness, their powerlessness. God compared us to a blade of grass or a flower out in a field. He said that not only is our human body frail, but our attractiveness, our kindness and our right behavior is also *temporary*. In other words, you are as weak and helpless against life as a blade of grass is under your foot! While you might pop back up when tread on, trouble can easily pluck you up, dig you up, crush you, or burn you up. That is the reality of our vulnerability. No wonder relationships wound us so easily!

By facing this reality of your own powerlessness, you can allow God to be strong in your life. You are weak, but God is invincible, all-powerful, and He is on your side. What keeps *you* from accepting this reality? There are probably many reasons you can consider. One common reason is shame. We are ashamed to be weak or vulnerable because we believe that we aren't *supposed* to be that way. We are supposed to be strong! All the cool people are strong, after all. This was part of the deception from Satan in the Garden of Eden. He convinced Eve and Adam that the only consequence of disobeying God was more knowledge and equal footing with Him. He *forgot* to mention the consequences of shame and fear. The reality of weakness makes it necessary for us to depend on God, through faith. The fear of shame can block you from admitting your weakness.

Shame and Blame. Paul writes about his own vulnerability and weakness in 2 Corinthians 12:9-11 when he was talking about praying and asking God to "remove a thorn in his flesh". This was something that obviously made Paul feel vulnerable, weak, and probably ashamed. He writes, "Each time he said, 'My grace is all you need. My power works best in weakness.' So now I am glad to boast about my weaknesses, so that the power of Christ can work through me. That's why I take pleasure in my weaknesses, and in the insults, hardships, persecutions, and troubles that I suffer for Christ. For when I am weak, then I am strong". At the beginning of the chapter, he talked about an amazing and miraculous vision he had, but then added in verse 5, "That experience is worth boasting about, but I'm not going to do it. I will boast only about my weaknesses." Paul had discovered the irony of vulnerability and rejected the shame of weakness. You too can reject the shame and *embrace* weakness so that God can be strong in your life.

Blame is a common reaction to shame. After Adam and Eve sinned, they both felt shame (Genesis 3) when they became aware that they were naked and had broken God's only rule. When God asked what happened, Adam blamed Eve and God. Eve blamed the serpent. The point of Stage 1 in Strategic Trauma and Abuse Recovery© isn't to blame your parents, your ex-husband, your Uncle John, or anyone else for that matter. This stage is actually about *taking responsibility* and *owning your wounds*. While it's not your fault you were wounded—someone else did that to you—it is, as I said in the last chapter, *your* problem. The wound is inside of *you* and *you* must own it and take responsibility for it in order to begin the healing process. Grieving is not about blaming others or about blaming yourself. It's about facing the reality of your wounds, your losses, and their location—inside of you.

Job is a great example of a complex but Godly reaction to trauma and loss. Job was an innocent man, very successful in business and a wise counselor. He had adult children who were really into partying and a wife who really enjoyed his riches. In the span of one day, Job lost nearly everything. He lost all of his children and all of his riches. His response was to take responsibility, to own these losses rather than ignoring them, silver lining them, or looking for a way to avoid the pain of them. He humbled himself, acknowledged his weakness and powerlessness, and waited on God. Job 1: 20-22, "Job stood up and tore his robe in grief. Then he shaved his head and fell to the ground to worship. He said, "I came naked from my mother's womb, and I will be naked when I leave. The Lord gave me what I had, and the Lord has taken it away. Praise the name of the Lord!" In all of this, Job did not sin by blaming God."

The next day, Job lost his health when he broke out in large, oozing sores. He also lost the respect of his wife. Job 2:9 "His wife said to him, 'Are you still trying to maintain your integrity? Curse God and die.'" She, like most people at the time, assumed that he must be guilty of some sin to bring all of this on himself. Of course, that wasn't true. All of these awful things came from Satan. "10 But Job replied, 'You talk like a foolish woman. Should we accept only good things from the hand of God and never anything bad?' So in all this, Job said nothing wrong." Job didn't deny that he was wounded, didn't deny that things were really bad, and didn't deny that he was grieved. He also didn't blame himself for the loss and trauma, nor did he blame God. Instead, he humbled himself and turned to God, waiting for His response.

Three friends traveled a long way to comfort and console Job. "12 When they saw Job from a distance, they scarcely recognized him. Wailing loudly, they tore their robes and threw dust into the air over their heads to show their grief. 13 Then they sat on the ground with him for seven days and nights. No one said a word to Job, for they saw that his suffering was too great for words" (Job 2: 12-13). Job accepted their comfort, but defended himself when they also began to blame him, telling him that this trauma must be his fault. You can express the attitude of Job when you admit that you, too, have an actively bleeding wound and accept that you are powerless over the wound, the wounding, and the one creating the wound.

VULNERABILITY

One fear that people express when asked to admit that they are wounded and accept their powerlessness is that this will lead to being unsafe, making them more vulnerable than before. If the reality is that you are vulnerable to being hurt, pretending you aren't isn't going to make a difference. Depending on God is safe, depending on ourselves is not. God can see the future, so only He can truly determine what is safe and what isn't. We can easily be fooled into thinking that something we choose to do is safe, like the puppy at the beginning of the chapter, when it isn't. Eve thought that knowledge would make her like God and would be a safe thing (Genesis 3:5b). Look where that landed her and us!

Growing up with childhood trauma, neglect, or adversity makes it more difficult to distinguish between a safe relationship and an unsafe relationship because you have been desensitized. Your compass has been reset and it doesn't point to true north. In fact, what you think is not safe, may be from God and have a purpose. To that effect, James, the half-brother of Jesus, wrote in James 1:2-4, "My friends, be glad, even if you have a lot of trouble. You know that you learn to endure by having your faith tested. But you must learn to endure everything, so that you will be completely mature and not lacking in anything."

An example of something in my life that I thought was unsafe, but turned out to be from God, happened several years ago. I received a threatening letter from someone who formerly claimed to be a friend and mentor saying he was suing me and that I had to stop doing the training and counseling I was doing immediately. That letter had the effect on me that he wanted it to have; I was terrified! I panicked! I spent hours, days, and weeks writhing in pain and fear on the inside. Outside I was irritable, short-tempered, and listless. How could this happen? I thought. I've done everything right! I've even promoted this person to everyone I've spoken to while training. After visiting several attorneys, I felt no better than before. At the time, I felt extremely unsafe. I prayed and asked God, "Please show me something to re-assure me of your presence." He did, more than once. Nevertheless, I continued to be afraid.

Over the next couple of years, God led me through a grieving and letting-go process that, in turn, led to the writing of this material. First, I had to give up on the dream I had of being a great leader in the field of psychological trauma recovery using the method I had become so adept at implementing, teaching, and understanding. While I wasn't happy during this process, now I see that I was never actually *unsafe*. God was directing my path all along. What this man meant for evil in my life, God used for good! It was another opportunity for me to see my powerlessness, my shortsightedness, and my weakness; an opportunity to contrast my weakness to God's power, omniscience, and strength; another opportunity for me to take my eyes off of my persecutor and put my eyes on my protector; my true source of safety: Him. Another opportunity for me to become aware that I was pointing my cup at that man, that method, and my success and turn it, instead, toward God my true source of love, acceptance, worth, and security.

POWERLESS VS. HELPLESS

When some people hear the word "powerless", they immediately rear-up inside. In fact, people found an addiction recovery organization in response to A.A.'s use of the word powerless. These people don't believe they are powerless over alcohol and instead want to learn to master its consumption. You, too, may not want to accept that you are powerless over the trauma wound, the wounding, and especially the one creating the wound. Let's talk a little about what powerlessness is and what it isn't.

To be powerless over the wound means that you can't heal it yourself. You can't will it away, nor will it to heal any more than you could will away a kidney stone. If you have ever had a kidney stone, you know the excruciating pain they cause. You can try to will that stone to move and pass out of your body all you want to, and believe me I have tried on more than one occasions, but it's going to pass when it passes. You might drink a lot of water, or take some medication that might ease the pain, but it will still be taking its sweet time moving through your system. You are powerless over that kidney stone! Like a kidney stone, you are powerless over the wound of trauma. You have to go through the process of healing; you can't just will it away.

You are powerless over the wounding. You didn't cause it and you didn't control it. Wouldn't you have kept it from happening if you could have? Of course! You are also powerless over the one who created the wound. Continuing to argue, replay the event in your head repeatedly, or figure out why it happened are all ways of trying to take control over the wounding or the perpetrator. You can't. *It is a fruitless endeavor.* You will never know "why". You will never find an explanation that takes away the pain or makes sense to you, even if it makes sense to the perpetrator. Trying to find the "why" is a common response, but it's like being on a giant hamster wheel. You keep going round and round and ending up right back where you started—wounded.

Being powerless over the wound doesn't mean you are powerless over everything and it doesn't mean you are helpless. There are many people around to help, if you ask. God wants to help. This program can help. You have the power to decide when you are ready to move through these stages, when you are ready to make the next step. You can make decisions to feed your faith, to find safer relationships, to take the steps toward healing. You have a lot of power. People who make this step, accepting they are powerless over the wound, the wounding and the one creating the wound find it paradoxically empowering! Surprisingly, admitting you are powerless over this one thing gives you a lot more power over the rest of your life.

Asking God for help is always a great place to start. Later in the first chapter of James' letter he wrote, "If any of you need wisdom, you should ask God, and it will be given to you. God is generous and won't correct you for asking." Have you ever asked a question in a class or a meeting and been given a response that clearly implied, "You should have already known the answer to that, dummy! *We* already know the answer, why don't you?" What did you feel? Stupid? Inadequate? Foolish? Did you decide never to ask another stupid question; to just keep your mouth shut and act as if you know exactly what everyone is talking about, even though you are clueless? Obviously, James had experienced that, because he assumed that the people he was writing to at the time had also had that experience. He reassures them that God is NOT like that. He says that God is generous. He wants to share His wisdom with us. He knows we don't know, and He won't get after us, look down on us, chastise us, or mock us for not knowing and for asking. A student in one of my classes wrote on the discussion board that his impression of Christianity was that the Bible discouraged people from asking questions. *This is so wrong!* The Bible is clear that you can ask God whatever you want. He is generous. He *wants* to share.

A great example of really understanding the difference between powerless and helpless is Joseph (Genesis 37, 39-41). He continued to experience trauma after trauma! First, at 17 years old, his jealous brothers ganged up on him, beat him up, and planned to murder him. One brother intervened and suggested throwing him in an underground tank to die. His brother suggested that because he intended to come back later and rescue Joseph. When he returned, however, the other brothers had changed their minds and sold him to a band of slave traders that were traveling to Egypt.

Once they arrived in Egypt, the traders sold Joseph to Potiphar, the captain of the palace guard. More trauma! While he was powerless to do anything about being a slave, he used the skills he had to do what he could, all the while trusting God to take care of him. God didn't rescue him from slavery, but He did prosper him where he was. Evidently, he was a very attractive young man and the wife of his boss began to sexually harass him, attempting to seduce him and threatening him if he didn't comply. Even more trauma! When she got very aggressive one day, he ran away leaving his outer garment behind him. She then accused him of rape. Since he was a slave, they threw him immediately into prison with other palace prisoners; they didn't give him a trial. What incredibly unfair trauma!

Genesis 39:21-23 tells us, "But the Lord was with Joseph in the prison and showed him his faithful love. And the Lord made Joseph a favorite with the prison warden. Before long, the warden put Joseph in charge of all the other prisoners and over everything that happened in the prison. The warden had no more worries, because Joseph took care of everything. The Lord was with him and caused everything he did to succeed." This wasn't magic and it wasn't a miracle. Joseph did what he needed to do by participating, by doing his part, by not spending energy trying to get out of prison, but by accepting his powerlessness while recognizing that he wasn't totally helpless.

Sometime later, while in prison, two other prisoners arrived and had dreams that Joseph interpreted. Joseph interpreted the dreams correctly, and didn't take credit for the interpretation but gave the credit, rightly, to God. Both of these men were direct servants of the Pharaoh and had access to him. Pharaoh beheaded the baker in prison, and the wine taster returned to work but forgot all about Joseph and the promise he made to help him get out of prison. For another two years, Joseph remained in prison and continued to do what he could, even though he was powerless to get out. Finally, when the Pharaoh had some dreams that needed interpreting, the previously imprisoned wine taster remembered Joseph. Then, the miracle came. The Pharaoh released Joseph from prison and made him second in command over all of Egypt, directly reporting to him. Joseph still gave God the credit and didn't take the credit for himself. He remained humble even then. Joseph saw and accepted his powerlessness without giving into helplessness.

While you are powerless over the wound of trauma, over having been wounded by trauma, (it's not your fault it happened) and over the one creating the wound, or perpetrator of the trauma, you are not *helpless*. Like Joseph, you are not *without help*; you *can* help your-self and you *can* ask for help. Look around you right now. What are you doing to help yourself? For one, you are reading this book. You are beginning to try to understand what happened to you and how it happened. In addition, you are looking for the pathway to healing. I hope that you are also feeding your faith in God by thinking about what you are reading, maybe discussing it with others who are on this journey or have made this journey, and using simple prayer to ask God to heal you.

FEEDING YOUR FAITH BY READING ABOUT GOD

Obviously, Joseph was doing something to feed his faith and so was Job, and they didn't even have a Bible to read like we do. In the last chapter, I presented one way of feeding your faith, Simple Prayer. Another way you can feed your faith is by reading the Bible. Maybe you look at the Bible and feel overwhelmed by its size, so you quit before you get started. Understanding the Bible's purpose and makeup can help, as well as reading one that is a normal book size and not a dictionary size.

While we view the Bible as one "book", it's actually a compilation of writings, including historical texts, poetry, prophesy, and letters. While the stories of Joseph and Job are from the Old Testament, the New Testament is a great place to start when your focus is feeding your faith. Reading about Jesus' life and ministry, as well as letters written by apostles (people who actually saw Jesus face-to-face) that explain Jesus' teachings, is very helpful in this endeavor.

Do you have 20 minutes a day to spend reading? Maybe 10 more minutes each day to spend thinking about what you read. If you will spend 30 minutes a day, (the length of time it takes to watch one comedy show like, "The Big Bang Theory") you can read the entire New Testament in only 60 days! If you doubled that and you spent 60 minutes a day reading and reflecting, (the length of time it takes to watch one drama like "CSI" on television) you could read the entire New Testament in only 30 days. You can find various plans at BibleGateway. com or on theBible.com/App to read or listen to on your phone.

Another thing that stops people from reading the Bible is their difficulty understanding the language. Both of the internet-based resources I mentioned have multiple languages and translations so that you can pick one *you* understand. You are supposed to be able to understand the Bible. When the writers wrote the various parts, they wrote in the common language spoken by people at the time. Don't treat it like Shakespeare's plays that you are required to read in the Old English when studying them in school. NO! Thousands of people have spent millions, probably billions, of hours translating the Bible texts from their original language into languages that all people can understand. They have been tortured, dismembered, and killed so that you can read it in your own language and understand it. You don't have to do the translating! Read it in a translation that makes sense to *you*.

Personally, I enjoy reading the New Living Translation. It's written with an American English structure and is available in other languages, too. It's easy to understand and the sentence structure flows well. I can still look up words, if I want to, and use other study Bibles. I use it for my everyday quiet time to feed my faith in God.

Think of it this way, if you had possession of a powerful pill that could cure you of all diseases but, instead of swallowing it, you carried it around and listened to other people talk about the impact taking it made in their lives, how much good is that pill going to do for *you*? NONE. No good at all. While reading the Bible won't cure you of all diseases, it will *transform* you, change you, and feed your faith in God in an *immeasurable* way. However, like the pill, you have to get it in you! You can't just carry it around and think about it or listen to other people talk about it. You have to read it. Then, read it again. Read it again. And then, read it again. Each time you will understand more and your faith in God will grow.

Keep moving forward on the pathway to healing that this program, Strategic Trauma and Abuse Recovery© has laid out for you. If you aren't fully onboard with accepting the fact that you are powerless, or when a desire to prove your strength raises its ugly head inside of you, make the intentional choice to keep moving toward acceptance inch by inch. A place to start is by acknowledging God's existence and considering that He might be for you, not against you. Read the Bible for yourself and find out if I am telling the truth. Start NOW.

CHAPTER 3 SUMMARY

1. Living in the pain of your wounds from trauma may be familiar to you, and you may interpret that as safe because that's all you've ever known. However, God wants to use this program as a way of uprooting you from that spot and rescuing you from an unsafe place to take you to a more abundant life.

2. Traumatic experiences launch us into the river against our will. You find yourself flailing around and trying to get back to the bank, to safety. You didn't choose this river, it seems to have chosen you. Now your only decision seems to be how to navigate the river.

3. There is a lot to learn about trauma recovery from river rafting. Having a guide makes the journey safer than doing it alone

4. When someone throws you into the river of trauma, behavior that seems logical for survival may not be the best move. Let someone who has navigated the river of trauma before lead you through safely.

5. The first stage of recovery is a reflection of the reality you find yourself in: I admit that I am wounded and I am accepting that I am powerless over the wound, the wounding, and the one creating the wound.

6. The more my perception overlaps with reality, the saner I am. Rather than trying to change reality to match perception, wisdom says we need to change our perception to match reality.

7. Our misperceptions keep us from trusting and obeying Christ,

therefore keeping us from knowing God. Trauma creates and feeds these misperceptions.

8. Facing the reality of trauma means making yourself emotionally vulnerable and emotional vulnerability is the most accurate measure of courage. The reality is, you are vulnerable, even if you think you aren't.

9. Even God sees you as weak and vulnerable and His reality is the truest. By facing this reality, you can allow God to be strong in your life.

10. While weakness and vulnerability are reality, shame blocks us from admitting or embracing this reality. You can reject the shame of weakness and embrace it so that God can be strong in your life.

11. A common reaction to shame is blame. Job is a great example of a complex but Godly reaction to trauma and loss. He embraced his weakness, rejected the shame, and didn't blame himself or God.

12. Only God can truly determine what is safe and what isn't. We can easily be fooled into thinking that something we choose to do is safe, when it isn't.

13. Growing-up with childhood trauma or neglect makes it even more difficult to distinguish between a safe relationship and unsafe relationship.

14. To be powerless over the wound means that you can't heal it yourself. You can't will it away or will it to heal any more than you could will away a kidney stone.

15. You are powerless over the wounding. You didn't cause it and you didn't control it. You will never find an explanation that takes away the pain or makes sense to you, even if it makes sense to the perpetrator.

16. Even though you are powerless over the wound, you are not powerless over everything and you are not helpless. When you

need help, you can ask God and those He has put in your life as guides to help you.

17. You can continue to move toward acceptance of powerlessness by acknowledging God's existence and considering that He might be for you, not against you.

18. God has wired the ability to heal into your DNA; following this plan activates the natural healing process already built into you. God will also provide guides to ride the raft of recovery with you—your facilitator and/or counselor. Participating in an organized S.T.A.R. program provides not only a map to follow, but also a group of friends to travel with you on your journey to recovery.

19. Start acceptance by considering that God is for you and not against you. Feed your faith in God by reading the Bible.

CHAPTER 4:
STOP TRYING
TO FIX YOURSELF!

"To acknowledge your imperfections does not mean you are a failure; it is an admission that you're human."

Gary Chapman

PERFECTIONISM

Ok I admit it, I'm a perfectionist. You may not believe me if you looked at my desk, covered in papers and notes and books and magazines. Nevertheless, I am a perfectionist. When I first started as a counselor back in the early 1980's, I was really gung-ho, about psychology and reading everything I could get my hands on. A person recommended a popular book to me, one I can't remember now, and I started reading it. I remember sitting in my car one day outside of a Publix and struggling with some of the concepts in the book. Reading it, I felt so inadequate, so overwhelmed, and so hopeless. I thought I'd never be able to change like that. "God," I pleaded, "please help me!" Maybe you think I'm crazy, but He answered me, not out-loud, but in a still small voice inside. He said, "Who asked you to change this about yourself?" Hmm, I thought. "I guess I did," I responded. "If I wanted that changed, I'd change it," He said. "I'd tell you to work on it. Stop trying to change yourself and let me work in your life." I started crying tears of relief. "I don't have to fix myself, I don't have to be someone I'm not," was my realization. Honestly, in my pursuit of perfection, I keep forgetting that.

Perfectionists just like me fill our world. There are more self-help books, blogs, tweets, and websites than I can count. We all want to be perfect and we all have a different definition of what perfect really means. Ask yourself, "If I were to fix myself, what would that mean? What would that look like? What would I look like?" and you will get an idea of what your concept of perfection is. Personally, I consider Jesus to be perfection. While I wouldn't be male, I wouldn't dress in a robe and sandals, and I wouldn't travel around speaking—not on foot, anyway—I'd have His heart for people, His faith in His father, and His courage to fulfill His mission regardless of the circumstances. The Christian church calls the process of becoming gradually more like Jesus in these ways, *sanctification.*

Sanctification requires transformation. Transformation means going through a gradual change, like a caterpillar to a butterfly. It's slow and invisible, but an amazing change. Paul wrote, "Don't copy the behavior and customs of this world, but let God transform you into a new person by changing the way you think. Then you will learn to know God's will for you, which is good and pleasing and perfect", (Romans 12:2). Notice he said, "Let God transform you." He didn't say, "Transform yourself."

This transformation takes place after you have been spiritually born again (salvation) and is an ongoing process in a Christian's life. Without salvation, change is nice, but temporary. No matter how much plastic surgery you have, some day you will die. Everyone dies, so physical change is temporary and all physical healing is temporary. The only change that is permanent is change to the part of you that will go on living forever, to your spirit, identity, or soul. If your spirit is dead, then change to your mind, will and emotions is still good for your life on this Earth. However, it is restricted because everyone must die. If your spirit is alive, then sanctification, change to your identity, mind, will and emotions will also last forever. God does the transforming, but you have to participate.

Trauma survivors have special needs when it comes to transformation because there are so many roadblocks set up in the brain due to the traumatic experiences. Don't let trauma block you from participating in God's transformation process. Trauma myth #2 is one of those roadblocks to transformation that I am going to address now. I believe it is a particularly heinous and cruel myth.

TRAUMA MYTH #2

I addressed the first myth about trauma in chapter 1, "If it happened when I was a child, it doesn't affect me anymore." Now, I want to address a common myth about God and discuss how it applies to trauma. I'm sure you've heard this before, "God will never give you more than you can bear." It's everywhere! However, the most important place that it isn't, is in the Bible. Not only is this NOT in the Bible, it is a potentially very dangerous and corrosive myth. While one author calls it "Sentimental Christianity,"[45] I think it is much more sinister than that. In fact, I think this is a myth circulated by the Enemy himself. Much like he did with Eve in the Garden of Eden, he took God's true words and twisted them to use against people and keep them from experiencing the healing or transformation God has for them.

This myth seems to be a misinterpretation of 1 Corinthians 10:13 which reads, "The temptations in your life are no different from what others experience. And God is faithful. He will not allow the temptation to be more than you can stand. When you are tempted, he will show you a way out so that you can endure." In this passage, Paul is writing about temptation to sin, not trials or tribulations. He is saying that we are all tempted to sin; the temptation to sin that you are experiencing is no different from the temptation that others face. We all want more, more money, more power, more beauty, and more fame. He adds that God is faithful to provide a way out of temptation so that you can endure the temptation. This has nothing to do with trials, tribulations, adversity or trauma!

In fact, many passages say just the opposite of this myth. Jesus said, "I have told you all this so that you may have peace in me. Here on earth you will have many trials and sorrows. But take heart, because

I have overcome the world" (John 16:33). He didn't say *you* will overcome the world, He said, He has overcome the world.

Examples of Biblical champions experiencing more than they can bear are numerous! Elijah was a real champion. In 1 Kings 18, we read about an amazing victory that Elijah spearheaded over the 450 prophets of Baal. They had a face-off and, after God showed His presence, proving He was real and Baal wasn't, Elijah killed all of the prophets of Baal with the people's support. Then, God once again proved His sovereignty by ending the drought in Israel, sending a massive rain from one tiny cloud. In chapter 19, when Queen Jezebel found out about it, she threatened to kill Elijah the next day. Terror overcame him and he ran in panic and begged God to kill him! After such an amazing victory, he was terrified by the threat of imminent death and I'm sure he was shocked by her refusal to see the truth about Yahweh God. Elijah ran to God's mountain for help, and God helped him.

When he arrived, God asked him, "What are you doing here, Elijah? 10 Elijah replied, "I have zealously served the Lord God Almighty. But the people of Israel have broken their covenant with you, torn down your altars, and killed every one of your prophets. I am the only one left, and now they are trying to kill me, too." I find this particular passage of scripture very intriguing. Elijah was honest, he despaired for his life and he told God what he perceived as the truth, as bad as it sounded. God took this opportunity to show Himself to Elijah. He showed Elijah His true nature and Elijah worshiped Him. God asked him the same question again. Sort of like in research, we do a pre- and post-test following a psychological intervention. Guess what?

Elijah's response was the same. Exactly word for word the same! After seeing and experiencing God's true nature up close and personal like that, he still had the same despair. Now I could spend a lot of time on Elijah and why or why not he responded the way he did, but my real focus here is on God's response to Elijah. God didn't scream, yell, become exasperated, insult him, throw him away, no. God calmly explained the truth. Elijah wasn't alone. God gave him some tasks to complete, including anointing his new protégé, Elisha, and Elijah went on his way. To sum it up, God protected him, gave him a protégé, and later sent a flaming chariot to escort Elijah to heaven. Elijah had much,

much more than he could handle. Nevertheless, God was faithful, respectful, and accommodating. WOW!

Another person from the New Testament that had more than he could handle was the Apostle Paul. In 2 Corinthians 1:8-10, Paul wrote to the church members in Corinth, "We think you ought to know, dear brothers and sisters, about the trouble we went through in the province of Asia. We were crushed and overwhelmed beyond our ability to endure, and we thought we would never live through it. In fact, we expected to die. But as a result, we stopped relying on ourselves and learned to rely only on God, who raises the dead. 10 And he did rescue us from mortal danger, and he will rescue us again. We have placed our confidence in him, and he will continue to rescue us."

Paul and his companions were not overwhelmed because of their own sin; they had done nothing wrong. In fact, they were doing everything right. The abuse they experienced in Asia was so overwhelming, so crushing and terrifying that they thought they were going to die, they expected to die. This adversity, these insults, these attacks drove them past relying on themselves to relying only on God. It is because of this kind of adversity that Paul developed the attitude of, "For to me, living means living for Christ, and dying is even better" (Philippians 1:21). Paul admitted openly that he and his Christian friends had much more than they could bear. He also knew that God knew about this and still had faith in God. He didn't expect any different.

Even Jesus, when He was hanging on the cross, beaten, exposed, and dying was overwhelmed and had more than He could bear. This is evidenced by His crying out from the cross as recorded in Matthew 27:46, "At about three o'clock, Jesus called out with a loud voice, "Eli, Eli, lema sabachthani?" which means "My God, my God, why have you abandoned me?"

There are several reasons why this myth is dangerous. First, it encourages complacency. People who believe this may not try to get out of a traumatic life situation, assuming that God just expects them to put up with it, and bear it. This is not true! Jesus vanished more than once when a crowd attempted to mob him. He left and went somewhere else, and He encouraged His disciples to "shake the dust off their feet and move on" (Matthew 10:14) when a town or community wasn't open to hearing the Good News about His salvation.

Second, it blames God for traumatic experiences. Most traumas in this life are due to people's selfish desires, lusts, greed, and sin. God doesn't sanction or promote sexual, physical, verbal and emotional abuse, for example. Psalms 11:5 says that God hates violence.

Third, when people are told, "God will never give you more than you can handle," and they believe it, then they compare it to their life experience or the life experience of others, they feel betrayed, abandoned, or experience doubt in the Bible's relevance. People logically assume that either the Bible is lying, or something is wrong with me. People then blame themselves, think that they are different because they can't handle this tragedy. You may become bitter with God, thinking that He's picking on you. Elijah, Paul, and Jesus did none of these things because they knew the truth. You will always have more than you can handle because that's what happens in our world—tragedy and trauma are inevitable.

There are several conclusions you can draw regarding trauma from all of this evidence. 1. You are not supposed to be able to bear the burden of trauma alone. Remember, as we talked about in Chapter 3, you are weak and frail, like a fragile flower or a blade of grass, and that is okay! That is who you are and how God created you. 2. Your pain is not evidence of your imperfection, its evidence of a wound that needs to heal. If you didn't feel pain, it would be like having emotional leprosy. The lack of pain is not the answer. 3. Trying to fix yourself isn't working, and never will. If you are like me and all the other trauma survivors in the world, you've tried lots of remedies to heal the pain, numb the pain, and avoid the pain. They don't work. This isn't a reflection of your imperfection, just a reflection of trying the wrong solution. 4. God can heal the wound of trauma if you let him. If you let Him, is the key.

STAGE 2

Stage 2: I have decided to give up trying to fix myself and I will humbly seek healing from God (or you can say my Higher Power), while fully understanding that healing will require my participation.

Let's review the wording here. "I have decided to give up trying to fix myself." This is not about giving up all of your survival responses. In fact, you probably aren't even aware of many of them, yet. Trying to eradicate your survival responses at this point is just another way of trying to fix yourself. Together, we are digging deeper than survival responses. We are going to the root of the trauma, the memory of the actual events that created the wound. Right now, you are gathering your tools, bracing yourself, and preparing to get to the roots. Ironically, when working through this stage with a few clients, I've had to ask them to STOP going to certain Bible studies because the focus of the study, much like the book I referred to in the story at the beginning of this chapter, was on changing yourself rather than God changing you. You are refocusing your attention on God, which the next part of this stage reflects.

In Mark 5, there is a story of a woman who had concluded that she had no other options left but to ask Jesus to heal her. Jesus was on his way to the home of Jairus, an important leader in a local synagogue to heal Jairus' 12-year old daughter who was dying. By this time, Jesus' fame had spread through the area and a throng of needy people was surrounding Him, pressing in on Him and blocking His path. One woman was different from the others, however. The author records that for 12 years she had constant bleeding which was probably vaginal bleeding. According to Mark 5:26, "She had suffered a great deal from many doctors, and over the years she had spent everything she had to pay them, but she had gotten no better. In fact, she had gotten worse." This woman was suffering physical pain, exhaustion, emotional trauma, and social rejection. Because of the bleeding, the laws at the time considered her "unclean". This meant she couldn't touch or be touched by anyone without causing them to also be considered unclean. The people considered Jesus a great teacher or rabbi and she especially should not have been touching Him in her "unclean" state.

However, she had evidently made the decision I am describing in this stage. She had given up on trying to fix herself and was asking God to heal her. She pushed into the crowd and got as close as she could to Jesus and reached out and touched just the hem of His robe. She didn't have the courage to get in His way and to ask Him face-to-face to heal her, like Jairus had. She preferred to stay anonymous. Her faith was present, though, however small it was, and Jesus knew the intent of her heart. I imagine the crowd being like you see at a Black Friday sale in Walmart where 500 people want to get to a stack of 10 computers for sale for $100 each. People were nearly stampeding Jesus. Even with all of this activity around Him, after *she* touched his robe, He stopped and turned around to the crowd and said, "Who touched my robe?" His disciples were flabbergasted. "What are you talking about, Jesus? Many people are touching you constantly. We can hardly get through this crowd as they are so pushy!" Jesus held firm, though and waited.

Why everyone didn't say, "It was me!! Heal me!!" I don't know. Only this woman came and fell down to the ground on her knees in front of Him, trembling, crying, and said, "I did it." Jesus didn't rebuke her for touching Him in her unclean state, nor did He ignore her and just go on about His business. He made her healing public rather than keeping it secret. When she used the courage and hope she had left to come forward, He responded with, "Daughter, your faith has made you well. Go in peace. Your suffering is over." I sincerely wish that emotional healing happened as fast as physical healing, but it usually doesn't. Turning to God through faith, however, can boost your hope in healing immediately.

HUMILITY

After making the decision to stop trying to fix myself, the next part of this stage reads, "will humbly seek healing from God". I'm asking God to do the healing or the fixing, but humility is the prerequisite to a successful ask. God doesn't owe you healing, you don't get to demand it, and He's not a gumball machine you put your quarter in and get your prize out. While you can approach Him with confidence, you also have to approach Him with humility. Perhaps that is why Jesus insisted that the woman with the issue of blood come forward rather than hiding in the crowd.

Humility means modesty, meekness, to have an unassuming nature, and is the opposite of arrogance. Spiritual growth requires humility. God spoke to Solomon in the new temple in 2 Chronicles 7: 14

and said, "Then if my people who are called by my name will humble themselves and pray and seek my face and turn from their wicked ways, I will hear from heaven and will forgive their sins and restore their land." James 4:9-10 says, "Let there be tears for what you have done. Let there be sorrow and deep grief. Let there be sadness instead of laughter, and gloom instead of joy. Humble yourselves before the Lord, and he will lift you up in honor." Jesus said, "But those who exalt themselves will be humbled, and those who humble themselves will be exalted," (Matthew 23:12). Also in Matthew 18:4, He said, "So anyone who becomes as humble as this little child is the greatest in the Kingdom of Heaven." Humility is a start, but still just the beginning of the process, however.

At some point in our lives, we all become aware of our own imperfections. Imperfection, intentional or unintentional, is sin. When faced with this realization, you have two choices; you can respond with an attitude of arrogance or you can respond with an attitude of humility. If you choose an attitude of humility toward God, this will lead to true repentance, true remorse for your sin and an admission of your guilt. True repentance takes place on the inside but leads to change of some kind on the outside. After all, you can't truly repent of sin and continue to participate in that behavior, attitude, or thought. This ongoing *transformation* leads to an increasing participation in the life of God (or a churchy word we use is *holiness*) and to an *increasing* awareness of your own imperfection or sin. This is valuable because it increases the overlap of your perception with reality, gradually shifting your perception of who you are to be more in line with your perception of how God sees you. It's important to note that you become MORE aware of your imperfection as you move closer to God, not less aware.

In order to tolerate this increased awareness, however, you must also become more aware of God's grace and mercy. Without this increased awareness, you *will* move to the choice of arrogance. This requires the catalyst of feeding your faith in God through activities like simple prayer and Bible reading. In chemistry terms, a "catalyst" is an agent that provokes or speeds significant change or action. In relationships, it means a person or thing that precipitates an event. While the act of praying or reading the Bible doesn't change you, many people study the Bible and don't even believe in God, when you mix it with belief in God and humility, your faith will grow. You don't earn God's grace by doing these things, you become more aware of it because you are more aware of Him. By adding these catalysts, you are making yourself available to God and He does the changing inside of you that, eventually, shows up on the outside.

ARROGANCE

If you don't intentionally choose humility, then you will naturally chose arrogance. If you choose an attitude of arrogance toward God, this leads to justification of your sinful or imperfect behavior, which of course means no change. This justification of sinful behavior leads to an increasing separation from the life of God (the churchy word we use for this is worldliness), and to a decreasing awareness of your own imperfection or sinful nature. Continuing this cycle leads you further and further into spiritual death, with less and less awareness of the problem.

The catalyst for this cycle is behavior that feeds your faith in something other than God. Things like feeding your faith in yourself through "self-help" programs designed to focus on your personal strength and power, not God's. Feeding your faith in alcohol, drugs, sex, pornography, education, domination, and your personality all serve to keep you stuck in this cycle of spiritual death. Notice that many of these things actually require and encourage a change, maybe even, what appears to be positive change, in your outward behavior. Many of them don't look like sinful behavior, like education, and seem to be a good thing to do. It's not the behavior itself that is the problem, it is just the catalyst. It's the change that the catalyst is sparking—increasing your faith in something other than God.

Remember the point is not legalism in your behavior. The point is that God changes us from the inside out and we simply have to make the choice between humility toward God, or arrogance. However, don't be deceived by your own outward behavior. Humility and arrogance are both about the heart. Good things can look like humility, but really be covering an attitude of arrogance. Let's look at an example from the Bible.

Naaman was a man who almost missed God's healing because of his arrogance. You can read the story of Naaman in 2 Kings 5:1-14. He was a very powerful military leader under Ben-Hadad II, the king of Aram-Damascus, in the time of Joram, king of Israel. The Bible says that the Lord had allowed Naaman to be very successful in his military career and he had advanced to be the commander of the Syrian army. Everyone loved Naaman, it seems, but he had the terrible skin disease of leprosy. The Bible doesn't tell us how advanced his disease was at this time. He was obviously still living with his family and going about his business. However, eventually the disease would advance far enough to disfigure him and cause him to have to live in isolation.

In one of the raids on Israel, the Syrian captured a young girl and gave her to Naaman's wife as a household slave. This young girl is an amazing and unsung hero of the story of Naaman. The soldiers took her from her home as a child and forced her to live in slavery in another country. They probably tore her from her mother's arms crying and screaming, or perhaps she even watched her mother beheaded by the long sword of a Syrian warrior. I picture her to be about eight or nine at this point; wearing a freshly scrubbed slave's tunic and ponytails. We don't know how long she had been there, but it couldn't have been too long since she was familiar with the current prophet in Israel, Elisha. She evidently came from a family that believed in God because she knew and had faith in Him and in His prophet. Somewhere inside of this little orphaned and kidnapped girl, however, were strong faith, love, and forgiveness.

When her master, Naaman, came down with leprosy, the whole family and servants must have been talking about it. Naaman was a wealthy and powerful man. He was also honorable and evidently treated his family and slaves well. If society exiled him, he would lose his place in the command of the army and with the King; therefore they would all lose their place of belonging and the advantages of living with his wealth, power, and prestige. Therefore, Naaman wasn't the only one who would lose as leprosy ran its course. Boldly and confidently, the little servant girl expressed her concern to Naaman's wife one day and said, "I wish my master would go see the prophet in Samaria. He would heal him of his leprosy," (vs 3). She passed the message to Naaman, appearing to practice humility by taking direction from a slave girl, and he spoke to his boss, King Ben-Hadad II. Both of them were hopeful that this might be a solution, so King Ben-Hadad II wrote a letter for Naaman commending him to King Joram of Israel, which read, "With this letter I present my servant Naaman. I want you to heal him of his leprosy," (vs 6).

There must have been a temporary peace between the two kings at this time, since he even thought to send the letter, but the message terrified King Joram. He tore his clothes in dismay and said, "This man sends me a leper to heal! Am I God, that I can give life and take it away? I can see that he's just trying to pick a fight with me," (vs 7). King Joram's faith was obviously lacking. He didn't even think of contacting Elisha. Somehow, however, Elisha heard about it and sent a message to King Joram saying, "Why are you so upset? Send Naaman to me, and he will learn that there is a true prophet here in Israel," (vs 8b).

Naaman, again appearing to be humbling himself, went to see Elisha with an entire entourage of horses and chariots, along with gifts to present for his services. Elisha, however, was not impressed with Naaman's station, power, or wealth and saw right through his false humility to his arrogant heart. Elisha pushed that button! He pushed it hard. He didn't even go out of his house to greet Naaman. He simply sent a messenger out to tell Naaman, "Go and wash yourself seven times in the Jordan River. Then your skin will be restored, and you will be healed of your leprosy," (vs 10).

Naaman was furious! He felt insulted by Elisha's offhand treatment and by his suggestion to dip in the Jordan River. Naaman wanted magic, he wanted Elisha to wave his hand over the leprosy and make it go away. He wanted respectful treatment befitting his station in life. He wanted Elisha to be impressed because that is what impressed him—prestige, belongings, and power. He certainly didn't expect to have to *participate* in the healing process. Fortunately, his officers talked some sense into him. Even though his initial response had been arrogance and, probably as usual, he into a rage, he calmed himself down, truly humbling himself on the inside and putting his faith in Elisha's God. Then he went and did what the prophet told him to do. Because of that, because of choosing humility toward God over his initial response of arrogance toward God healed Naaman of leprosy.

There are several examples of humility in this story. The servant girl demonstrated humility. She could have held her tongue, knowing that healing was waiting for Naaman in Israel, but angry over Naaman's troops kidnapping her and forcing her into slavery. Naaman's wife demonstrated humility. She could have scolded the girl and told her to keep her mouth shut! Naaman demonstrated a measure of outward humility when he listened to his wife and the servant girl, when he went to King Ben-Hadad II, and when he presented himself to King Joram. Naaman demonstrated true humility catalyzed by desperation, when he listened to his officers, and then listened to Elisha. He returned to Elisha to thank him and said, "Now I know that there is no God in all the world except in Israel," (vs 15). He also offered Elisha gifts of gold, silver, and 10 suits of clothing. Elisha demonstrated humility and said, no I won't take them, still not impressed by Naaman's wealth. Naaman also vowed to serve only the Lord in his heart from then on.

Some people demonstrated arrogance, too, however. King Ben-Hadad II demonstrated arrogance in his letter demanding that King Joram heal Naaman. King Joram demonstrated arrogance when he assumed it was all up to him and didn't consider even asking God or Elisha for help. Notice that what many may interpret on the outside as humility was actually arrogance. His assumption was he was the most powerful person there was and if he couldn't do it, it couldn't be done. See how that is actually arrogance? Naaman's hidden arrogance was exposed when Elisha didn't come out of his house. He demonstrated this hidden arrogance when he became enraged. Naaman's arrogance almost cost him everything. Because Elisha didn't treat him in the way he had become accustomed to being treated, he thought it was ridiculous to dip in the river, especially seven times. He almost didn't do it. Nevertheless, he decided to *humble* himself and do the work of participating in the healing that God had for him.

Your Current Understanding of God

Because none of us has seen God face-to-face yet, we come to understand God based on our experiences. Because our experiences and the cultures in which we grow up are diverse, our understanding of God, even if we read the Bible and believe what it says, are diverse.

However, as we get to know Him better, we get a clearer understanding of who He really is and our understandings, regardless of our diverse backgrounds, begin to converge. For example, I went on a youth trip when I was in the 9th or 10th grade from our home in Piper, Kansas to the mountains of Colorado. I imagined the pioneers driving across the flat plains of Kansas. We could see the horizon; the land is so flat and treeless. Eventually, as you progress westward, mountains appear on the horizon. Not everyone could see the mountains, and they looked very different, depending on your eyesight and the part of the van or car in which you were sitting. If I held up my pointer finger and thumb in a measuring sort of way, and looked at the mountains through the space, they looked like they were about an inch high. "No problem!" you might think, "I'm big enough to get over that."

As you get closer, the mountains grow, but you stay the same size. Now they are a foot high, then three feet, and then four. Eventually, when you get to the base of them, however, you get a true idea of just how big they are as you compare them to your puniness. Standing at the base, you may not even be able to see the top, let alone comprehend how you are going to get over them. That's how it is with God. When you are far away from Him, He looks small, unimportant, and easily overcome. Far enough away, in fact, you can't see Him at all and may believe He doesn't exist. Still, this is just *perspective* and not *reality*. As you get closer to Him, you begin to see His magnitude, His awesomeness, His power, and His size in comparison to yourself and your wounds.

True humility is recognizing and accepting who God is in comparison to you. Perhaps you are as I was when I was still miles away from the mountains and they looked so tiny. You are far away from God and, while you think He is probably there, maybe you think He's not interested, or big enough, or caring enough to think about you and your pain. That is the starting point from which you can seek healing for your wounds. From the perspective you *currently* have of God, whatever that perspective happens to be. You don't have to be a super-saint, or an evangelist, or a radical. You just have to look out over the horizon and open your eyes and see that there is *someone* there. As you move closer, God will appear bigger. Before you know it,

He'll appear to be bigger than you. Of course, He never changed. He's always been that magnificent. You just got close enough to see the reality of Him.

I love the study of science, especially psychology. Psychology only shows us our problems, though. The New Covenant in the New Testament shows us our solution. Psychology helps us to understand human problems, why they exist, what they look like, and how common they are. The Bible helps us to understand God and His remarkable solutions to our human problems.

My Participation in Healing

This brings us to the last part of this stage, "...while fully understanding that healing will require my participation." God does the healing, but you *have to participate*. It does require something of you. Perhaps it is not what you think it should require. Naaman, for example, had to dip himself in the river. The woman with the issue of blood had to break the rule of touching the rabbi when she was unclean, and then she had to have the courage to admit to everyone that she did it. It would be nice if emotional healing was magic and someone could just wave his or her hands over you and poof! All of your emotional pain would be gone along with all of the long-term impact of the traumatic experiences. Unfortunately, healing from trauma and adversity doesn't work that way.

Eventually, in Phase Two, the "Reprocessing and Grieving" Phase, you will need to talk about the events in detail, identify your contradicted expectations, emotions and losses. Then you will be able to identify how you interpreted the experiences and implemented changes in your thoughts, behaviors, attitudes and values. Right now, you are preparing for that phase by feeding your faith so that you can find true safety in Christ. Working through the stages, one at a time, will move you deeper into your healing. You just have to keep moving.

Feeding Your Faith through Worship

So far, we've talked about two main ways of feeding your faith:

Simple prayer and Bible reading. <u>Another way to feed your faith is through worship.</u> What is worship? In modern <u>Christianity, it seems to be limited</u> to music, but really, it's an attitude of adoration and submission to God. <u>King David and the other writers of the book of</u> Psalms practiced worship through songs, poetry, music, and writing. You can express your attitude of adoration and submission in many ways including music, poetry, kneeling, praying, serving, or even writing letters to God. However, it is an attitude and doesn't require any specific posture or tools to practice.

Earlier in this chapter, I used the illustration of driving across the plains toward the mountains and watching the mountains "grow". The mountains aren't really growing, it's our perception and visual vantage point that is changing. As we move closer to God, He isn't growing either. Instead, we are seeing Him more clearly for whom He *really* is. This is the whole point of feeding your faith: to continue to see God more clearly for who He really is. One of the things I do to try to experience God is to use my imagination. When I participate in corporate worship through singing, I close my eyes and imagine Jesus listening to the songs, smiling, and singing along with us. One song we sing describes running into the arms of God/Jesus and I imagine being a little child running toward my dad, wanting him to pick me up so he can swing me around. I imagine kneeling down at Jesus' feet and having Him lift me up to face Him while He smiles at me and cups my face in His hands. These are all very intimate moments for me and sharing them with you is, honestly, a little difficult. During these times of listening and singing, I try to imagine the song as a way of talking to God. That might mean laughing with Him or crying with Him. I know God enjoys being with us while we sing, laugh, and celebrate His goodness. However, for many trauma survivors, this is a difficult task. If you had an abusive or absent father, it may be difficult to imagine God as kind or even present. We've also been fed images of God being like an old grandfather, angry at us, and unapproachable.

One of the things that helped me was to watch a video called, *The Visual Bible- Matthew* directed by Reghardt van den Bergh. It's available on DVD or direct download from Amazon.com and was released in 2004. There have been several movies produced about Jesus and in most of them, the actor portrays Him as very serious and speaks in old English as if He lived in Elizabethan times in England and was perpetually solemn and annoyed. Bruce Marchiano, however, portrays Jesus in a friendly, attractive, and happy manner. There are several wonderfully moving scenes where he laughs, smiles, cries, and plays around with people. Watching this movie, which is word-for-word from the book of Matthew in the NIV translation, brought a three dimensional aspect to scripture that I had never experienced before! Jesus seemed more real, alive, and approachable! I really wanted to be friends with this guy! I wanted to follow Him! By the closing credits when Jesus is walking along the seashore and turns to the camera with a big smile on his face and motions to come follow him, I was on my feet and in tears, ready to go. You can see the closing scene posted on youtube.com here: https://www.youtube.com/watch?v=9E_jq8scNxM.

Another one of my favorite scenes is from Matthew 8 where a leper approached Jesus and his disciples and asked to be healed. He said, "Lord, if you are willing, you can heal me." Jesus gets down and says, "I am willing". Jesus doesn't just walk away, He celebrates with the man, hugging him and even falling on the ground with him laughing. You can watch the scene here: https://www.youtube.com/watch?v=H7o-J3SDmVTA. Use your imagination and put yourself in this man's place. Jesus *wants* to heal you; He's *willing* to do it! I wish that emotional healing happened in the same way physical healing happened when Jesus was on Earth, it doesn't seem to. It's a process, but Jesus is just waiting for you to ask. Use worship to feed your faith in Him and His desire to heal you.

CHAPTER 4 SUMMARY

1. Perfectionists fill our world. I know I'm a perfectionist, and you are probably a perfectionist, too.

2. True perfection, for Christians, is being more like Jesus.

3. Sanctification is the process of becoming gradually more like Jesus, and requires transformation.

4. Transformation is going through a gradual change, like a caterpillar to a butterfly. It's slow and invisible, but an amazing change.

5. Transformation takes place after salvation and continues until death. Without salvation, all change is only temporary since everyone dies.

6. God does the transforming, but we have to participate.

7. Trauma survivors have special needs when it comes to transformation because of the lies set up in our minds by the perpetrator. These create roadblocks to transformation.

8. One of those roadblocks is trauma myth #2, "God will never give you more than you can bear". This is a sinister myth propagated by the enemy himself that says God did this to you, and you are on your own.

9. Many Biblical champions had more than, on their own, they could bear. Including Elijah, Paul, and even Jesus.

10. Trauma myth #2 is dangerous because 1. It teaches complacency; 2. It blames God for traumatic experiences; 3. It promotes bitterness toward God and division in the body of Christ.

11. God can and will heal the wound of trauma and Stage 2 is all

about letting him: I have decided to give up trying to fix myself and will humbly seek healing through God while fully understanding that healing will require my participation.

12. Deciding to give up trying to fix yourself is not the same as giving up all of your survival responses. We are going deeper than that! We are going to the memory of the event that created the wound in the first place.

13. The "woman with the issue of blood" written about in Mark 5 is a great example of someone who made the decision to stop trying to fix herself and ask Jesus to heal her.

14. When faced with the realization of your own imperfection, you get two choices; you can respond with an attitude of arrogance or you can respond with an attitude of humility.

15. Humility allows ongoing sanctification in our lives, arrogance keeps us stuck justifying our behavior and in a cycle of spiritual death.

16. Naaman (2 Kings 5) is a great example of someone who almost missed his healing because of his arrogance.

17. You get to start wherever you are in your understanding of God. Right now, he may seem small, distant, and uncaring. As you move closer, God will appear bigger. Before you know it, He'll appear bigger than you.

18. Emotional healing isn't magic. Healing requires YOUR participation and, in Phase Two: the "Reprocessing and Grieving" Phase, you will need to talk in detail about the events that wounded you. Right now, you are preparing for Phase Two by feeding your faith so that you can find true safety in Christ.

19. Another way to feed your faith is through worship and using your imagination.

CHAPTER 5:
NAVIGATING
THE WILDERNESS OF GRIEF

"No one ever told me that grief felt so like fear. I am not afraid, but the sensation is like being afraid."

C.S. Lewis

"The only thing we have to fear is fear itself—nameless, unreasoning, unjustified terror which paralyzes needed efforts to convert retreat into advance."

Franklin Delano Roosevelt

THE IMPORTANCE OF REMEMBERING

I grew up in California around the San Francisco Bay area. When I was growing up, we called my dad "The Great Pathfinder". We called him this because, bless his heart, he was always lost. My mom and dad loved to take us camping and their favorite place was a little logging town called, Ruth. A friend of my parents' owned the town and the logging company that worked the area. My dad worked full-time for Chrysler and was a part-time preacher. He had friends who owned automotive dealerships and loaned him motor homes to take on our trips. This one particular year, I was probably in the fifth grade, around 10 years old, and we were driving in a motor home to the village of Ruth, California. It was late and dark and we were driving in a huge, heavy, motor home through slick, muddy, unpaved roads to an unknown location. My mom, my brothers and I were scared and, though my dad was lost, he was determined to get us to where he wanted to camp. We were literally on the side of a mountain driving on roads cut for the logging trucks to get in and out with the timber. Finally, we seemed to get down off a peak and into a valley that was level enough for us to stop and park for the night. My dad drove out into the middle of the valley, as close to the river as he could get, so that he could hear the water running. He didn't get out and look around, he just parked and we all went to bed.

The next morning, my mom was the first one up. She opened the door to go outside and screamed, "Jack! Jack! We're in the middle of a river!" I also ran to the door. Sure enough, we were in the middle of a wide, shallow, river! The bottom was small stones with maybe 8-10 inches of clear, ice-cold mountain water rapidly flowing under and around our motor home.

It took a few hours, but eventually someone towed us out of the river and onto dry land. Then we were on our way. Remembering is important. If my dad had remembered his way, perhaps we wouldn't have been lost. If one of my parents had remembered to go outside and check the perimeter, perhaps we could have moved out of the river right away and not lost a day on our vacation. Nevertheless, it was a family adventure none of us has ever forgotten nor let the Great Pathfinder forget.

There are times when forgetting can be helpful, you forget a lot every day. While research shows that your brain may actively work to erase what it considers unimportant details, maybe cell phone numbers, or where you put your car keys, where you parked your car, etc., your brain considers traumatic memories very important because they involve survival. Therefore, the brain is more likely to be move them to long-term storage where they continue to live-on. Just because they are stored, "in the background" doesn't mean they don't affect what's going on in your body, however, especially when they are revisited over and over again. Even traumatic memories that are only triggered occasionally impact the brain because of the domino effect.

You make a decision is based on the traumatic experience, which leads to another decision, and another decision. Soon, you're not sure why you are doing what you are doing, but at one point it made sense.

A well-known analogy is the following: A woman was preparing Christmas dinner and teaching her daughter how to cook a ham. She proceeded to cut off both ends of the ham and place it in a pan to bake. The daughter asked, "Mom, why did you cut off all of that good meat from the ham?" She paused and said, "I don't know. That's what my mom taught me to do, so that's what I do." The mom, now perplexed by her own behavior, went to her mom (the grand-mom) and asked, "Mom, why did you teach me to cut off good ham on each end at Christmas? It seems so wasteful." The grand-mom paused and said, "Well, that's how my mom taught me to do it, so that's how I've always done it." As it happened, her mom was still alive, so the grand-mom went to her mom (the great grand mom) and asked, "Mom, why did you teach me to cut off both ends of the ham. That's good meat!" Her mom, the great grand mom said, "Well honey, I didn't have a pan big enough back then so I had to cut off both ends to make it fit." The "tradition" of cutting off both ends of the ham made sense when it started, but the conditions had changed. Continuing with the behavior didn't make sense anymore, but it continued to be passed down to the next generation, until it was challenged. Then, they had to get to the root of the problem so they could adjust their behavior to fit the current circumstances. This is the same thing that happens with trauma in our individual life and how frequently survival responses are handed down to the next generation, actually now functioning to create more problems rather than solving problems.

TRAUMA MYTH #3

Another common myth passed own in Christian circle is, "God doesn't want me to look back and grieve over the past. Grief is a sign that I don't have enough faith. He wants me to forget it and press forward to the future." A secular version is similar, "Forget about the past and just focus on the present, that's all that matters."

The secular version seems to be rooted in Stoic Philosophy, which is at the root of Cognitive Behavioral Therapies.[46] There is in fact an entire theory of psychology, Reality Therapy or Choice Theory, that believes considering the past is a waste of time and not helpful. I used to find this model very attractive. The problem is, because a brain transplant isn't possible, and because the present builds on the past, your past always affects your present, and your present always affects your future. Sure, you can make different choices now than you did then, but the past has changed your brain and if those changes aren't acknowledged and addressed directly, they continue to hold power over the present, even if you aren't consciously aware of this happening.

Another challenge to this approach is that psychotherapy is about facilitating change. People want to change their behavior, which changes their relationships, their circumstances and their life. If considering the past, identifying the connections between the past and the present for an individual isn't important, why do we spend so much time on remembering the past at the global level? Why do we insist that our children learn history, study the past, and be able to visit museums that contain relics and proof of the past? Put simply, because the past is important.

We need to know where we as a people-group come from so that we don't repeat the mistakes of the past. Continuing to educate people about the holocaust is an important example. Even in our "modern" era, there are young people who are "holocaust deniers".[47] These people believe that the Holocaust never happened. They say that it is either a gross overestimation, exaggeration or flat out lie that 6 million Jews, and another approximately 5 million gay people, priests, gypsies, people with mental or physical disabilities, communists, trade unionists, Jehovah's Witnesses, anarchists, Poles and other Slavic peoples, black people and resistance fighters, were systematically rounded up and murdered.[48] Even though there are museums, structures like Auschwitz still standing, people deny that it happened. Amazing.

The Christian version of this myth seems to come from Philippians 3:13: "No, dear brothers and sisters, I have not achieved it, but I focus on this one thing: Forgetting the past and looking forward to what lies ahead, I press on to reach the end of the race and receive the heavenly prize for which God, through Christ Jesus, is calling us." Context is always important when interpreting Scripture, and this verse, when taken out of context, does appear to be endorsing forgetting your past. However, if you back up to the beginning of the chapter and to the previous chapter you will find that this passage is about righteousness in Christ rather than righteousness in our own works. In Philippians 3: 5-7, Paul recounts his achievements, but then says they are worthless for righteousness because true righteousness is in Christ. Paul is "forgetting" what he did in the past to achieve right-standing with God (the Law) because it is worthless and instead pressing on to know Christ more, finding his righteousness ONLY through his relationship with Christ. Paul also spends a lot of time recounting his many trials and adversities through his letters, debunking this myth that somehow forgetting the past demonstrates faith in God. It does NOT.

THE BIBLICAL MANDATE TO REMEMBER

In searching the Scripture, it was difficult for me to find any passage where God instructs His people to forget. Let go of other God's or lifestyles, stop following other Gods or false teachings, put away sinful behavior, yes, but forget your past? I haven't found that—yet. Perhaps someone will show it to me someday and I'll become convinced, but not yet. In fact, the Old and New Testaments are full of recorded memories of the past. Stories of failure and victory. Horrible stories of mistakes made and consequences experienced, as well as God's rescue and provision when people repent and turn to Him. Indeed, the Scripture contains many instructions to *remember*.

One specific passage about remembering is Exodus 12-13. In this passage, the people of Israel had survived the passing over of the Angel of Death in Egypt who killed all of the first-born sons of the Egyptians, both human and animal. God spared the Israelites because they followed His instructions to paint the blood of the sacrificed lamb on their doorposts. The Pharaoh kicked them out of Egypt and they began their journey to the Promised Land. Even before they reached the Red Sea, God gave instructions to Moses in chapter 12, and Moses turned around and gave the instructions to the Israelites.

In Exodus 12:14, God told Moses to tell the people, "This is a day to remember. Each year, from generation to generation, you must celebrate it as a special festival to the Lord. This is a law for all time." He then went on to give instructions on how to repeat in a ritualistic way all of the events of the last plague in Egypt when the Angel of Death passed over and killed the first-born sons. God didn't instruct them to forget about this horrible ordeal, forget about the bondage they were in and the entire trauma they experienced. God instructed them to remember that they were rescued and how. We know now that this is foreshadowing of the crucifixion of Jesus, God's only son. In order to make the connection, however, they had to remember and record all of the events and pass the information down in detail to their children and grandchildren from generation to generation.

Later in their journey, unfortunately, they did forget. In Numbers 11:4-6 you read, "Then the foreign rabble that were traveling with the Israelites began to crave the good things of Egypt. In addition, the people of Israel began to complain. 'Oh, for some meat!' they exclaimed. 'We remember the fish we used to eat for free in Egypt. And we had all the cucumbers, melons, leeks, onions, and garlic we wanted. But now our appetites are gone. All we ever see is this manna!'" The "foreign rabble" were probably Egyptians who left with them. Perhaps they weren't slaves, but married or befriended the Israelites. This complaining spread, though, and many of the Israelites picked it up.

There is a lot of untruth in their complaining. Nothing they ate was free; they were slaves! They paid with their lives and their children's lives. They paid with their freedom, their dignity, and autonomy. Slavery in Egypt was probably much like the slavery in America, brutal, cruel and dehumanizing. Any time one human being "owns" another, exploitation and degradation will take place. They seem to have forgotten that in this passage. In modern psychology, we call that "Stockholm Syndrome" or capture-syndrome. It's a psychological phenomenon in which hostages experience and express empathy or sympathy and may even have positive feelings toward their captors. Sometimes they even defend or protect their captors to the point of welcoming beatings from them. Perhaps this is what the Israelites were experiencing. They forgot the barbaric conditions under which they lived, including the murder of their babies. Perhaps if they had practiced remembering like God told them to, it might have spared them the consequences of forgetting.

INTENTIONAL REMEMBERING VS. ACCIDENTAL REMEMBERING.

While God's instructions were to remember on purpose, much of what trauma survivors remember is accidental. Of course, you do forget a lot of details, and even happy events. Scientists debate as to whether your brain permanently erased the memories, or if they are still there, just not easily accessed.[49,50] Accidental remembering happens when you put so much energy into forgetting traumatic experiences, but then they pop back up. I like to illustrate this like a beach ball you are holding under water. When inflated, the further you try to push it under the water, the more force the water exerts on the ball, making it difficult to push it further. Because the surface of the ball is slick, eventually you will lose your grip and it will pop to the surface. Traumatic memories are similar in that the more you try to push them below the surface of our mind, the more pressure you feel internally. Eventually you will lose our grip on our brain. Your memories will then pop "to the surface" where you have to deal with them or try to push them down again. This is actually one of the key symptoms of Post-Traumatic Stress Disorder, intrusive memories. Another PTSD symptom related to this symptom, is the triggering of past feelings and memories by current events or places. This is accidental remembering, not intentional.

God instructed the children of Israel to remember so that they could dwell not only on the pain, but also they could really appreciate the rescue and know who He is by His reputation. You can't separate one from the other; if you are going to celebrate the rescue, you have to remember the pain. If you are going to allow God to heal you from past or current/recent traumatic events, you have to intentionally remember and even focus or dwell on those memories.

In order to endure the memories, you must have faith that God knows what He is doing and that you don't have to walk through this alone. The Israelites who made it to the Promised Land made it because of their faith in God, not because of their fear of returning to slavery. That's why we are spending all of this time focusing on feeding our faith. God provided opportunities for the Israelites to feed their faith during their journey through the wilderness. Some took advantage of these opportunities and grew their faith, some just continued to live in fear and complain. It wasn't that the people who continued in faith weren't fearful, of course they were! Fear is a God-given emotion and is there for our own good. There are things we should fear. Instead, faith means we move forward while we fight through our fear. It may not go away, but faith in God's strength, power, and love for us overcomes our fear, even if it doesn't completely remove it. ✗

In Exodus 13:17-18, Moses wrote, "When Pharaoh finally let the people go, and God did not lead them along the main road that runs through Philistine territory, even though that was the shortest route to the Promised Land. God said, "If the people are faced with a battle, they might change their minds and return to Egypt." Instead, God led them in a roundabout way through the wilderness toward the Red Sea. Thus the Israelites left Egypt like an army ready for battle." God met the people where they were, with the amount of faith they had at the time. He didn't try to throw them into something they weren't ready for. That's what He wants to do for you.—to meet you where you are with the amount of faith you have. Eventually, when you are ready, we will get to the battle in Phase 2: Reprocessing and Grieving. There you will write and share your stories about your traumatic experiences. Now, focus on feeding your faith so that you can navigate the wilderness of grief successfully.

STAGE 3: THE VALUE AND IMPORTANCE OF GRIEF

Stage 3: I am accepting that I have to grieve in order to heal and I'm determined to allow myself to feel as I move through the healing process even though it will be painful and scary at times.

The two parts to this stage include accepting grief, and not trying to block the grief experience. At some point in church history, it seems that grieving became "ungodly," perhaps a sign that a Christian's faith is weak. However, the Bible doesn't support this. Many Christians teach that we must always smile; we should always act as if everything is fine, and that being a Christian means never having pain or sorrow. This leads to disappointment in God, deception, and putting on a false face. This is so far from God's plan or expectations for us.

In Matthew 23:37, we read about Jesus pouring out His heart with grief over Jerusalem. In John 16, Jesus prophesied to the disciples that they would grieve over His death; at least until He rose up from the grave. He didn't chastise them or tell them not to grieve. He said it matter-of-factly and plainly that they would grieve because there would be something to grieve about.

In Matthew 5:4, Jesus said, "Blessed are those who mourn because they will be comforted." This is from the Beatitudes. Jesus was teaching the ancient concept of being "blessed" by God rather than the modern concept of "happiness". We think of happiness as a feeling of satisfaction and pleasure. Jesus was saying that mourning our losses is an attitude that leads to blessing from God because it is only through embracing our grief that we can experience true comfort. In addition, the Apostle John calls the Holy Spirit, "The Comforter" in John 14:16 and 26.

In 1 Thessalonians 4:13, Paul wrote: "And now, dear brothers and sisters, we want you to know what will happen to the believers who have died so you will not grieve like people who have no hope." Paul acknowledges that we will grieve when people die, but that we can do so with hope because of the resurrection. If this principle applies to grieving the death of a loved one, it also applies to grieving other losses. We will grieve, but we can grieve with hope for healing, restoration, and ultimately heaven.

In John 11, we read the story of the death of a friend of Jesus', Lazarus. When Jesus came to the tomb, He knew He was going to raise Lazarus from the dead, but He wept anyway. Whether He was weeping with the people, or weeping because of their lack of faith in Him, isn't clear. Nevertheless, He was sad enough that He cried. He demonstrated grief, and yet He never sinned nor was He imperfect. Grieving isn't sin and isn't a sign of being imperfect or Jesus wouldn't have done it.

LOSS: THE TRIGGER FOR GRIEF

When people think of grief or grief counseling, they tend to think only about death. However, grief occurs over the loss of other things and the loss of people to things other than death, like divorce. Grieving the break-up of a marriage or dating relationship can be as painful as losing someone to cancer. In fact, it can be more painful because adding in the dynamics of personal rejection and ensuing sense of inadequacy. Therefore, as you are going through this recovery process, consider giving yourself permission to grieve as if someone had died.

All healing comes from God regardless of its appearance. This is because God is our creator and He wired healing for our body into our DNA. Nothing else heals itself like God's living creatures. Anything with DNA has the ability, to some extent or another, to heal itself. If someone isn't healing that would be expected to heal, we consider this an abnormality and another disease. Because God is consistent, my theory is that He also wired healing of the inner-self into the DNA of humans. God designed humanity to be resilient; not that we won't get hurt, but that we will heal when we do. Grief is a part of emotional and psychological healing. Moving through the process of grief is moving through the process of healing. Therefore, resisting grief is resisting healing. The problem happens when we are stuck in our grief or when we refuse to grieve.

Grief happens in stages and does not look the same for everyone, though there are some general patterns that most people follow. Grief can last a very long time so you can't put a time limit on it. You might experience delayed grief. When you don't realize you've lost something, you won't start grieving its loss until you know it's gone. If my car has been stolen, but I don't know it yet because I'm out of town, my grief won't begin until I recognize and accept the fact that the car is indeed gone. If I valued my car, then I will grieve its loss. If I was hoping someone would steal it so I could get a new one anyway, then I won't be grieving. Either way, the car was already gone; it was lost to me, even if I didn't know it.

This is how it is for some people abused as children. Physical and verbal abuse may seem normal. They may assume that everyone experiences emotional detachment and neglect. When sexual abuse starts from birth, they may not realize that what is taking place is abuse. It may seem normal, especially if the parent introduces the abuse in subtle and gentle ways, making it seem like fun and communicating, "This is what is supposed to happen. It's okay." The child may interpret this like a diaper change; uncomfortable, perhaps, but part of life. As the child grows, however, they become increasingly aware of themselves and their own bodies. They begin to doubt that this is right.

When the contradictions begin to move into awareness, so do the losses. There are tangible losses and intangible losses. For example, losses might include control, desire/will to live, dignity, femininity or masculinity, freedom, self-respect, self-confidence, self-worth, and much, much more.

Just like the stolen car analogy, people experience events differently and experience different losses. This depends on perception, personality type, past experiences, etc. There are some universal losses, however, which God wired into the brain based on universal needs. All human beings have basic physiological needs; safety needs, and emotional or psychological needs. One way you can remember these is to use the acronym, L.A.W.S. It stands for love, acceptance, worth, and security. I believe that all human beings have a need to be in relationship with God, also. As I presented earlier in the Trauma Survivor Blueprint©, contradictions to these God-wired expectations result in loss for people. The severity of the loss is individual, again determined by personality, circumstance, previous life experiences, etc.

What happens to many people who experience trauma is that you are stuck in grief. You can't move backward and make the loss not happen, but you are afraid to fully embrace it and move forward. On the other hand, perhaps you aren't aware that you are grieving over losses because you are trying to forget them or someone has led you to believe that you haven't lost anything. Therefore, you are stuck. You have lots of emotion, but you don't know what the emotion is about. That frequently leads to the conclusion, "I must be crazy!"

Let's briefly review the Trauma Survivor Blueprint© which I introduced to you in chapter 2. 1. An event outside of our conscious control contradicts expectations, needs, values or beliefs." 2. Your brain sees this event as a threat to your well-being and triggers the limbic system of your brain, the fight, flight, fright, fix part. 3. You experience losses and your grief response begins, meaning you have grief emotions. Losses can be things that are tangible and things that are intangible. Losing money, time, a person, etc. is tangible; you can touch these things and therefore they are easier to understand as losses. Things like a good time, safety, security, self-esteem, self-worth, hope, your image of a person, your view of life, etc. are intangible. You can't touch them or see them. They are internal experiences and therefore not as easily identifiable as losses.

Each traumatic event has its own set of losses, much as each bracelet you wear has its own set of beads. The thread that passes through the center connects the beads to each other. In the same way, an experience of trauma connects the set of losses together. Each loss then has its own set of grief emotions attached to the loss. Therefore, if I've had an experience of seeing my parents fight violently, for example, I may have lost security, respect, trust, and my image of how a husband and wife should treat each other. Each of those losses has its own set of grief emotions resulting from, and attached to, the loss.

At this point in the process, you could confront the perpetrator, resolve the traumatic experience, and your grief would be resolved. This requires participation of all parties involved in the event, however, including the perpetrator. If that happens, then the process doesn't move forward and the brain doesn't continue to revisit it, relive it, and give more and more power to the memory. However, if it's not resolved at this point, as time passes, because the brain is always organizing itself, similar emotions join together creating this cumulative emotional affect in your brain.[51]

Think of your brain like a coin-sorter. There is one opening at the top, and you drop in a handful of coins. The machine funnels quarters into one stack, nickels into another, pennies in another and dimes in another. Similarly, anger sorts with anger, hurt with hurt, sadness with sadness, etc. As these emotions "stack", the person experiences the accumulation of each emotion. Your anger grows, your hurt grows, your sadness grows, etc. Now, in the present, when you experience an emotion such as irritation, it sorts with anger and adds to the stack. Then, a person "overreacts" to the current situation. Anger escalates to rage; hurt escalates to a deep wound, sadness to profound grief, etc. In reality, the event activates all of the stacked anger at once; like a light string, when you plug in one light, they all light up![52]

When this escalation happens, maybe a part of you knows you are overreacting and you think, "I must be crazy!" People around you believe you are overreacting and they think, "She must be crazy!" Therefore, it increases the desire to just stuff the feelings, try to control them, or medicate them. However, this only serves to increase the accumulation of more saved up emotion. Tracing them to their source, and grieving the source, is the way to really experience healing. I hope that the following overview of grief, the process, the history and other people's take on grief will convince you of the need to grieve, and the possibility of moving through the grief cycle successfully. Until you move through grief and stop trying to avoid it or bargain it away, you will remain stuck. Embracing your grief is one of the most important steps to healing from trauma.

STAGES OF GRIEF

Elisabeth Kübler-Ross originally identified the Grief Cycle in 1969 as she observed dying patients and their families. The five stages identified by Kübler-Ross are denial, anger, bargaining, depression, and acceptance. In a book published posthumously, she wrote, "The stages have evolved since their introduction, and they have been very misunderstood over the past three decades. They were never meant to help tuck messy emotions into neat packages. They are responses to loss that many people have, but there is not a typical response to loss, as there is no typical loss. Our grief is as individual as our lives." The grief cycle, broken down into stages, serves as a framework to help us *understand* and *make sense* of our experiences following loss, not as a blueprint for resolving loss.

While grief isn't experienced exactly the same by everyone, there are some general stages that most people move through. Emotions are chemical, and universal, natural chemical changes take place in our brains and bodies when we have experienced loss, even the loss of feeling good. Kübler-Ross made her observations while working with families who had already experienced some loss with the diagnosis, but were also anticipating further loss. Anticipation can make things scarier, bigger, or in other ways larger than they are in reality. Following traumatic loss where anticipation is not present, however, for most people, the first stage of grief is shock.

SHOCK

General numbness and disorientation accompany this stage. Frequently, people describe feeling stunned and even dazed. To use a physical analogy; when the body experiences a physical trauma that creates blood loss, remaining blood pools in the center of the body, reducing flow and leaving the limbs with a reduction in oxygen and other nutrients required for functioning. This is called cardiovascular shock, Stage I; also, compensated, or non-progressive.[53] God designed this system perfectly to preserve your vital organs and systems, even if you have to sacrifice a limb. However, when shock progresses to Stage II or Stage III, doctors know something is wrong; blood is still being lost. With proper resolution of shock, the brain redistributes the blood out to the body in a normal and healthy way.

While physical shock and psychological shock are not exactly the same, with the onset of psychological trauma, emotions tend to "pool" in the center of the person, surrounded by shock and protected by denial. Following a rape, survivors tend to appear disoriented and easily suggestible, leading frequently to re-victimization. Even 10 or more years following a traumatic event, survivors still describe feeling stunned or shocked that the rape or other event actually occurred. Social psychologists suggest that shock happens because of the severe contradictions to survivor's expectations.[54] Nevertheless, since life must go on, people bury the incident in their memory, filing it away, and sometimes even forget or physiologically block it creating a form of amnesia.

DENIAL

In most cases, the second stage of grief, denial, sets in rather than amnesia, however. In this stage, the person has an awareness of the event, but minimizes its impact on their life. Denial allows people to continue living and protecting themselves from a recurrence of the event, while simultaneously protecting themselves from the pain of the losses caused by the event. This stage may last the rest of the person's life.

ANGER-TURNED INWARD

The third stage in the grief cycle for trauma survivors tends to be the anger stage. This may start out as anger turned inward, but, if the person isn't stuck in this stage, will eventually become anger turned outward, focused on the real perpetrator or source of loss. Inwardly focused anger takes the form of self-blame, shame, and guilt, and may even become depression. Some of this may be focused on some real responsibility, but much is focused on taking responsibility for things that aren't the survivors fault. Many childhood survivors blame themselves for sexual abuse, even though they were forced, manipulated, or coerced. This false sense of control works to help the person feel a false sense of power, but at the same time keeps them stuck in the grief cycle. Because they see themselves as responsible and internally blame themselves for something they did not really have control over, they respond on the outside as defensive and angry. While this may look like anger turned outward, the outward anger is a reaction to the internal self-recrimination.

ANGER-TURNED OUTWARD

As a person moves through the grief cycle, anger begins to turn outward over the increased awareness of what actually took place. As the reality of what took place moves increasingly into your awareness, you become increasingly appalled at the facts. The reality of lost innocence, security, self-worth, etc., creates more righteous anger, anger that is in balance with the reality of the situation. You may initially express anger in a more shotgun-like fashion; aimed at everyone and everything around you that might be pushing your boundaries of safety and security. As you work through some of the fear, the anger settles on the actual perpetrator and becomes a calm, laser-focused anger from which it is difficult to retreat.

BARGAINING

Once a person gets past this stage, it is rarer, though not impossible, for them to cycle back to denial. It is in this stage, however, that many people do become stuck and begin the bargaining process which takes them back to the stage of denial only to move forward to anger and back yet again. Emotionally, it resembles a hamster running on a wheel; the hamster is working hard, moving forward, exerting energy, but never leaves the same spot. He is stuck in its cage. Bargaining, when it comes to processing the grief of traumatic or adverse events, functions as an attempt to negotiate a different way of resolving the loss. In other words, because the grief is too painful, the brain wants to do something different.

This "something different" typically involves some way of taking control of the situation; this may be stoic resistance to the reality or may be anesthetization using drugs, alcohol, food, shopping, gambling or some other anesthetic of choice. This isn't always a conscious decision to bargain, though some people are more self-aware than others. Instead, it's the brain's way of protecting itself from the pain of loss. Bargaining behaviors are the same as survival responses. Unfortunately, bargaining can keep a person stuck for years on the "hamster wheel" of grief. In order to get unstuck, the advantages of grieving have to outweigh the advantages of avoiding the pain.

ACCEPTANCE OF THE PAIN

When you have successfully navigated through the anger stages, the fourth stage seems to be the Acceptance of the Pain stage. In this stage, you will experience deep mourning and grieving as the reality of the loss, both past and present, moves fully into conscious awareness. You freely experience and express sadness, anger, resentment, and other very normal grief emotions. However, now you are aware that they are connected directly to your losses and you aren't afraid of them. This stage lasts longer for some than others, depending on the number of losses and the severity of your experience.

RESOLUTION

The final stage of grief we will call Resolution. In this stage, you experience increasing peace with, and recognition of, the losses as well as post-traumatic growth resulting from the experiences. In this stage, you will view the event or events as experiences in the past that influence, but no longer control the present. You develop perspective on the events and accept them as a legitimate part of your life story, while no longer seeing the trauma as defining your life. Resolution does not mean that you no longer have any feelings about the event; but the feelings you do have are easily assessable, while not overwhelming; identifiable, but much less frequently triggered; openly expressed without fear and without overwhelming shame.

Successfully navigating through grief is important because it prepares you for moving on to the third phase of recovery, which is Reconnecting. Without the successful navigation, intentional reconnecting won't take place.

ALLOWING MYSELF TO FEEL

While the first part of Stage 3 is about accepting that I have to grieve, the second part is allowing myself to feel the grief. Scientists continue to try to understand feelings. Why do we have them, what are they for, and where do they originate are just a few of the questions researchers and Biblical scholars try to understand. While we don't know everything, we do know that everyone has feelings, even if they don't completely understand them. Feelings consist of various chemicals secreted from our brain and body that wash over the brain, thereby creating physiological responses throughout our entire system. We learn to interpret these different mixes of chemicals and give them names. The more you pay attention to our feelings, the more self-aware you become. Being self-aware doesn't mean self-centered. It means to be aware of where you are in relation to everything around you. This awareness allows you to connect with others, figure out who is safe and who isn't, and deal with problems as they come up rather than after they become bigger.

As stated previously, this process is NOT about changing yourself, but about allowing God to heal you. In order to do that, God leads us through a grieving process. Moving through grief is a reflection of the healing taking place on the inside. While there are innumerable survival responses people use to manage their painful feelings, there are two types of survival responses that block feelings and stop the grieving process in its tracks, thus keeping you stuck. These are stoicism and substance use.

STOICISM

This attitude of "stoicism" can become a life philosophy, if allowed to continue. Stoicism is a Hellenistic philosophy that originated in Athens in the early 3rd century BC. The Stoics taught that destructive emotions came from mistakes in judgment, and that a wise person, or a person of "moral and intellectual perfection", would not experience such emotions. In other words, the smarter you are, the less negative emotion you feel. In fact, they consider indifference in itself to be power.[55] This sounds similar to a modern Christian philosophy of the more faith you have, the less pain you will feel when you are injured. The more faith you have, the more you are able to ignore your past or present wounds and just move forward. While it may be unintentional, this path leads to invulnerability and indifference.

The Apostle Paul tangled with Stoic philosophers and Dr. Luke recorded it in Acts 17-18, "He also had a debate with some of the Epicurean and Stoic philosophers. When he told them about Jesus and His resurrection, they said, "What's this babbler trying to say with these strange ideas he's picked up?' Others said, 'He seems to be preaching about some foreign gods.'" Obviously, the Stoics of the time turned away from Christianity. A later Stoic called Christianity, "false hope". A famous psychologist, Albert Ellis, himself a stoic and atheist, built his model, Rational Emotive Behavior Therapy on the philosophy of Stoicism. He teaches people to take another view of traumatic incidents and therefore remove the negative feelings associated with it.[56]

When I am referring to stoicism in this context, I am not referring to self-control. Self-control is a "fruit" of the Spirit mentioned in Galatians 5:22-23. Paul said, "And "don't sin by letting anger control you." Don't let the sun go down while you are still angry." This type of self-control should be applied to all emotion; "don't let hurt control you", "don't let pain control you", etc. The philosophy of stoicism says there is NO value in painful emotions and numbing myself to them is the ultimate form of control. I've heard it expressed as, "FIDO", "Forget it and drive on".

If you secretly subscribe to this philosophy, you can go through this entire process, do all the writing in Phase 2, and still not heal from your hidden wounds. Until you are ready and willing to embrace your painful emotions, even if you don't fully understand how to do that or think it won't make a difference, you won't experience the emotional healing that God can bring through this process.

Letting go of stoicism takes practice. To begin, start by acknowledging that you have painful emotions and make a decision to allow yourself to feel them. You might write the decision down on a piece of paper or notecard, "I will allow myself to feel painful emotions." You may keep a "feeling's journal" or daily write down your feelings. Become a "surfer" with your emotions. What I mean is, much like the sport of surfing, you ride the waves of emotion, not letting them take you down, and not fighting against them, but working with them.

This is an important decision for you to make. Deciding to let go of stoicism is an ongoing decision. It's scary at first, because you don't think that you can survive the painful emotions of grief. Nevertheless, you can. You can embrace your emotions, feel them, process them, and allow them to dissipate naturally, in the manner in which God designed you to heal. While you don't have to identify and give up all of your survival responses, this one will keep you stuck where you are. Embrace your feelings and move forward in the grief cycle.

Sedating Substances

The second survival response that blocks emotions and prevents moving forward in the grief cycle is substance use. Not all substances block grief, but those that anesthetize the brain can keep your brain from healing, even if you experience grief emotions. Pharmaceutical companies have created many different kinds of medicines to anesthetize pain. I am mostly concerned about those that work in the brain rather than in the body. Those that work in the body, like acetaminophen or ibuprofen work in the body and don't interfere. Sedating substances might include benzodiazepines, opiates, marijuana, cocaine, any illegal drugs and most illegally obtained prescription drugs used to "get high". Giving up all alcohol and sedating substance use during the next phase of recovery is important to the healing of your brain.

WARNING: Consulting a physician before ending your substance use is VITAL. Sudden stopping of some substances (including alcohol depending on the amount you have been consuming) can have a negative and even life-threatening impact.

ALCOHOL

Although there are other sedating substances that block grief, one of the most commonly used substances is alcohol. A comprehensive discussion of the impact of multiple drugs is outside the design and purpose of this book. Since alcohol use is extremely common, that is the only thing we will address here. Society has typically discussed alcohol consumption from a moral perspective rather than a physical or neurological perspective. Moral views on the consumption of alcohol range from any consumption is sin, to consumption in any amount is acceptable. Researchers, however, are moving to viewing alcohol consumption more as a public health problem.[57] In the past, clinicians have viewed alcohol use as either responsible use or addiction. More recently, the developers of SBIRT (Screening, Brief-Intervention, and Referral to Treatment) have begun to define a new category: excessive use. They point out that excessive or risky use can lead to injury, trauma and trauma recidivism, causation or exacerbation of health conditions, exacerbation of mental health conditions, alcohol poisoning, DUI, date rape, domestic and other forms of violence, transmission of sexually transmitted diseases, unintended pregnancies and substance dependence.[58]

According to research, only 5% of people who consume alcohol actually become dependent on it, while a full 20% become hazardous drinkers suffering some serious consequences of their use.[59] However, regardless of whether or not you drink excessively, any amount of alcohol affects your brain by creating an anesthetizing affect and interfering with not only the grief process, but also supporting the philosophy of stoicism.

ALCOHOL USE AS A SURVIVAL RESPONSE

A common survival response or coping mechanism is the consumption of alcohol and other substances like cocaine, marijuana, prescription pain medication, or prescription benzodiazepines. People drink alcoholic beverages because of the way it makes them feel. They may not drink excessively, but alcohol in any amount crosses the blood/brain barrier, bonding on receptor sites in the brain and slowing the neuropathways, easing pain, anxiety, and stress. Depending on the amount consumed and the conditions of the person consuming it, short-term side effects include sleepiness, euphoria, dizziness, nausea, loss of motor coordination, loss of accurate perception—physically and psychologically--exaggerated emotional swings, anemia, breathing difficulties, black-outs, and coma. Binge-drinking or continued drinking in high-risk amounts has even more severe consequences. These long-term consequences might be:

1. Unintentional injuries such as car crash, falls, burns, drowning.

2. Intentional injuries such as firearm injuries, sexual assault, domestic violence.

3. Increased on-the-job injuries and loss of productivity.

4. Increased family problems, broken relationships;

5. Alcohol poisoning;

6. High blood pressure, stroke, and other heart-related diseases;

7. Liver disease.

8. Nerve damage.

9. Sexual problems.

10. Permanent damage to the brain.

11. Vitamin B1 deficiency, which can lead to a disorder characterized by amnesia, apathy and disorientation.

12. Ulcers; Gastritis (inflammation of stomach walls).

13. Malnutrition.

14. Cancer of the mouth and throat.[60]

Of course, most people know about many of these potential issues and choose to drink anyway. What surprises many of my clients, however, is the way it affects emotions and relationships. Alcohol crosses the blood/brain barrier, regardless of the amount or concentration you drink. A standard drink is any drink that contains about 0.6 fluid ounces or 1.2 tablespoons of pure alcohol. That really isn't much! Alcoholic beverages are diluted and flavored to different degrees. Therefore, a mixed drink could be equivalent to three or more standard drinks. Different brands and types of beverages vary in their exact amounts of alcohol, but here are some equivalents.

1-12 oz. beer = 1-5 oz. glass of wine = 1-.6 oz. shot of liquor

"Malt liquor" is higher in concentration than beer and 1-12 oz. bottle is one and a half standard drinks. A standard bottle of wine is 750 ml or 25 oz., or five standard drinks.[61]

When the alcohol crosses into the brain, the molecules bind on the receptor sites of the neurons where the natural chemicals should bind. These chemicals, serotonin, norepinephrine, and dopamine are the chemicals when, present in the right amount, cause us to feel normal and good. *Homeostasis* is the biological state of all chemicals being in correct and stable balance to each other. This is an important biochemical fact. God designed our brains to return to homeostasis should it ever be disrupted. External chemicals crossing the blood/brain barrier and binding on the sites reserved for the natural chemicals, especially in a massive quantity disrupts this natural homeostasis. This massive binding of alcohol molecules creates a state of euphoria, which we call "buzzed" or drunk. The brain is very sensitive and in an attempt to return to the stable state stops making the natural chemicals.

When you stop drinking, the alcohol molecules break down and cleaning cells remove them from the body through the blood and eventually the urine. At this point the brain is again out of homeostasis, this time below normal instead of above. While above normal is euphoria, the below normal is depression. This is a chemical depression, which is also emotional depression, and creates anger, irritation, anxiety, fear, and even sadness. The brain will now be compelled to create more chemicals to move the brain back up to normal homeostasis. For each minute the brain spends in euphoria, it will spend approximately three minutes in depression before returning to homeostasis.[62]

Research shows that men who drink more than four standard drinks in a day (or more than 14 per week) and women who drink more than three in a day (or more than seven per week) are at increased risk for alcohol-related problems. If you drink outside these guidelines, you should visit a certified addiction counselor and participate in a screening.[63]

The impact of alcohol consumption is not only physical, but also social and emotional. You may start your night out drinking a couple of drinks, having fun, enjoying your conversation, but fighting by the end of the evening. Alcohol consumption heightens trauma symptoms like anger, sadness, and fear. While you may not be addicted, alcohol consumption can still make things worse in your relationships and emotional well-being, in addition to blocking brain changing, healing grief.

THE BIBLE AND ALCOHOL

So far, I've talked about alcohol use considering only the physical, emotional, and relational impact, but the Bible has a lot to say about alcohol use, also. The New Living Translation of the Bible uses the word "drunk" 66 times. It mentions wine 235 times, as consuming wine was a common experience. In Genesis you can read a story about Noah getting drunk on wine. The story is presented as neutral, "One day he drank some wine he had made, and he became drunk and lay naked inside his tent."[64] However, the aftermath was not neutral. His son Ham saw him, looked at him, and told everyone else. His other sons covered him without looking at him, demonstrating respect for him and indicating the inappropriateness of his situation.

Later in the book of Genesis, Lot's daughters decided to get him drunk so they could have sex with him to get pregnant (Genesis 19:32-34). The first night, daughter number one had sex with him and the writer records, "He was unaware of her lying down or getting up again." It appears he was so drunk that he had a blackout. The next night, they repeated the same process with daughter number two. In both of these stories, the consumption of alcohol leads to some very negative relational consequences, including the exploitation of the person who was drunk. Noah lost his dignity, his relationship with his son Ham, and his grandson Canaan, who he cursed. Lot lost his dignity and his daughter's respect for him. Later, his descendants, though related to the Israelites, caused the people many problems.

In Ephesians 5:18-19, Paul wrote, "Don't be drunk with wine, because that will ruin your life. Instead, be filled with the Holy Spirit, singing psalms and hymns and spiritual songs among yourselves, and making music to the Lord in your hearts." I think it's interesting that Paul contrasts and compares the work of wine with the work of the Holy Spirit. Jesus called the Holy Spirit "the Comforter" because He brings us comfort. One of the architects of the ACE study, Dr. Vincent Felitti, describes chemical use as "unconscious although understandable decisions being made to seek chemical relief from the ongoing effects of old trauma, often at the cost of accepting future health risk."[65] In other words, people turn to substances for comfort and relief from the pain resulting from past trauma. Perhaps what Paul is saying in Ephesians 5 is, rather than turning to alcohol, turn to the Holy Spirit for comfort from your pain or discomfort.

MAKING A DECISION ABOUT
ALCOHOL AND OTHER SUBSTANCES

At this stage, many S.T.A.R. participants ask, "Do I really have to quit drinking ALL alcohol (cocaine, marijuana, prescription pain medicine, etc.)? Even having a Margarita with my Mexican food on Friday night?" The answer is that depends. If you want Phase 2 to be effective, total abstinence really is necessary. This is a physiological issue, not a moral issue. Research has demonstrated that talk therapy rewires the neuropathways of the brain.[66] Alcohol anesthetizes the neuropathways and prevents the rewiring from happening. While a person may be quite emotional even while under the influence, it interferes with the permanent, neurological changes that need to take place, including the return of the brain to homeostasis. "Cell-plasticity" is the ability of the neurons in the brain to move around and connect to other neurons. Alcohol consumption in any amount decreases cell-plasticity, decreasing the functionality of the brain. This doesn't require a person to be an "addict"; consumption in any amount affects the brain. When the Strategic Trauma and Abuse Recovery© process is completed through all six steps, you may return to drinking alcohol within healthy guidelines, should you choose. It's not forever or a lifestyle of complete abstinence. If you want more information, you can watch a great lecture on the biochemistry of the brain by Merril Norton at http://www.youtube.com/watch?v=e9F5wpvq2h0. As always, the choice is up to you.

EXPECTATIONS FOR CHANGE IN S.T.A.R.

The only change to your survival responses that I am suggesting you make prior to completing the Reprocessing and Grieving phase is stoic philosophy and substance use. Most other survival responses, except of course suicidal thoughts, behavior or self-harm, will be bypassed and allowed to resolve on their own as we move through the healing process. All change is self-change, takes place over time, and occurs gradually.[67] Researchers Prochaska and DeClemente, have identified stages which all people go through when making changes. These stages are:

1. Pre-contemplation: In this stage, a person has no awareness of any need to change and doesn't consider changing. Example: A person sees no need to stop drinking either through denial that they have negative consequences from drinking or using other drugs, or because they have concluded that drinking alcohol or using other drugs adds too much value to their lives.

2. Contemplation: In this stage, people are undecided, unsure, perhaps conflicted about changing. They are beginning to consider change and think about the advantages and barriers

to change. Example: People may think, "I know I need to stop drinking, but I can't." Or, "I know I should stop smoking, but I'm afraid that I will get too anxious or be in a situation where people will ridicule me for not using."

3. Preparation: In this stage, people begin to prepare for making a specific change. Example: A person may say to himself/herself, "Okay. I'm going to quit but I just don't know how." They then may begin to read books or articles about stopping their alcohol or drug use. They may go to A.A., Celebrate Recovery, or Victorious Living and begin to develop strategies for quitting.

4. Action: In this stage, people take action to make the change they have been considering. Example: A person may stop drinking or smoking suddenly; may reduce drinking or drug use, or may commit to treatment at a more intense level.

5. Maintenance and Relapse Prevention: This stage involves maintaining the desired change and attempting to prevent relapse into old patterns. Substance use example: A person may continue in a support group or continue in a trauma recovery process, like STAR© or something else, until the desire for substances is gone.

People are continuously cycling through these stages until the change they want to make becomes more or less permanent. Understanding these stages of change can be very helpful as you consider your choice between drinking alcohol and not drinking alcohol, between turning to the Holy Spirit, and turning to a substance. Weigh the benefits and the costs for yourself. Research shows that most people are willing to continue to use substances, even knowing the long-term health threats, for the short-term benefit of relief from the pain.[68] That is why faith in God is so important. Putting faith in a Higher Power will give you the courage to stop using the substances long enough to move through the healing process of Phase 2: Reprocessing and Grieving. If you choose not to stop using chemicals, including alcohol, you will remain in the more formal Safety Phase until you make a commitment to complete abstinence. You are still on the path to recovery…just not ready for grieving yet. That's okay.

You are where you are now, and when you are ready to move forward, God will meet you there.

Feeding Your Faith through Music

Music brings people together and it sets them apart. Some like Rock, others Classical, Rap, Hip-Hop, Country, New Country, Alternative--- and the list goes on! The words of a song, as well as the tempo and instruments used can change your mood. They can encourage you and give you energy, or discourage you and make you sad. They can be arousing and they can be nauseating. The power of music is fascinating! Mark Hall, of Casting Crowns wrote a song that he titled, "Until the Whole World Hears." It's his declaration that he and his bandmates will continue to sing until everyone has heard about God's goodness, grace, and mercy. Spend time listening to music which points to God, encourages you to focus on God, and talks about His healing. At the end of my classes, I usually play a youtube.com video that reminds the class participants of just those things. I ask them to listen to the words, maybe close their eyes and imagine what the words are saying is true, and write down what they have heard about healing from trauma that day. I know this goes along with worship, in some ways, but you can listen while you are commuting, while you are working in your cubicle, while you are cleaning, or while you are exercising. You can find lots of good music by listening to Christian radio locally or by satellite. Try it and feed your faith through music today while you pray, read, and worship.

Chapter 5 Summary

1. Forgetting can be helpful when it comes to unimportant details. Because traumatic memories are about survival and are emotionally charged, they tend to live on in the brain.

2. Just because memories are stored, "in the background" it doesn't mean they don't affect what's going on in the foreground.

3. Trauma myth #3 has a secular and a Christianized version. The Christianized version is something like, "God doesn't want me to look back and grieve over the past. Grief is a sign that I don't have enough faith. He wants me to forget it and press forward to the future."

4. The secular version is something like, "Forget about the past and just focus on the present, that's all that matters," and seems to be rooted in Stoic philosophy.

4. The Christian version seems to be a distortion of Philippians 3:13. Paul was talking about forgetting his accomplishments, not his past pain. He is pressing forward to faith in Christ to achieve true righteousness, not relying on his works.

5. The Bible if full of passages with instructions to remember, not to forget. One example is the establishment of the high holy day of Passover, which is a way to remember accurately God's rescue of Israel from Egypt.

6. Intentional remembering and accidental remembering are different. Accidental remembering happens when you put so much energy into forgetting traumatic experiences, but they pop back up. Intentional remembering is what God instructed the children of Israel to do.

7. God didn't instruct them to remember so that they could dwell on the pain, but so that they could dwell on the rescue and know who he is by his reputation.

8. Faith in God is what gets you through the difficulty, pain, and fear of remembering.

9. Grief is important and valuable. Jesus grieved. He taught that true blessedness—as opposed to the modern concept of happiness—involves mourning to receive comfort.

10. Paul taught that grieving was natural and normal, and that we can experience grief and hope at the same time.

11. God wired you to heal and moving through grief is moving through healing. Therefore, resisting grief is resisting healing.

12. Loss is a common experience, but is determined by the individuals own identity. Each traumatic event results in multiple losses and separate grief emotions accompany each loss.

13. What happens to many people who experience trauma is that you are stuck in grief. You can't move backward and you can't move forward. You have lots of emotion, but you don't know what the emotion is about. That frequently leads to the conclusion, "I must be crazy!"

14. The impact of trauma is cumulative and emotions stack-up like coins in a coin sorter.

15. Grief happens in stages and doesn't look the same for everyone, though there are some basic stages. These include Shock, Denial, Anger turned inward/Anger turned outward, Acceptance of the Pain, and Resolution.

16. Two common survival responses directly block grief. These are stoicism and sedating substances.

17. The most commonly used sedating substance is alcohol. Other sedating substances, which will interfere with the natural healing of trauma, include benzodiazepines, opiates, marijuana, cocaine, any illegal drugs and most illegally obtained prescription drugs used to "get high".

18. Quitting all alcohol and sedating substance use during the next phase of recovery is important to the healing of your brain, but are the only two survival responses you have to change before continuing into the next phase of trauma recovery.

19. Consulting a physician before ending your substance use is VITAL. Sudden stopping of some substances (including alcohol depending on the amount you have been consuming) can have a negative and even life-threatening impact.

20. Listening to music which points out the goodness of God is another great way to feed your faith.

CHAPTER 6:
PARTNERING FOR HEALING

"Healing begins when you do something. God's help is near and always available, but it's given to those who seek it. Healing starts when you take a step. God honors radical, risk-taking faith."

Max Lucado

In 1992, I had a successful outpatient private practice in Houston, Texas. I had also started a Christian inpatient program with a psychiatrist business partner at a local psychiatric hospital. I was working with a Christian client who was dealing with a husband who was a crack addict, she and her children were living with her in-laws and he was living on the street, but in and out of the house. We had been working together for a few months and I was using basic Rational Emotive (Behavioral) Therapy, which was my go-to counseling model at the time. We worked on boundaries, trying to change her reactions with him, and detach from his addiction. It wasn't working. Either she couldn't do the interventions I was suggesting, or he changed the rules of the game. One day she said to me something like, "Denice, I really like you and you've helped me a lot. But I'm really stuck and I don't know what to do."

I looked at her, grateful she had told me and not just quit counseling, which is what most clients do, and said, "I agree with you. You are stuck. Truthfully, I don't know what to do about it. But I know that

God does know what to do, so let's pray and ask Him to show us." Since she was a Christian client, prayer was a part of our weekly session, so I felt comfortable doing this and she agreed. We prayed and waited.

The next day, the woman in charge of marketing for the hospital I worked with called me and insisted I attend a weeklong workshop about trauma recovery. It was a new model and gaining popularity in that area and she wanted me to connect with them and draw in patients to the hospital. I didn't want to go because it meant giving up an entire week of revenue! However, I owed her, she twisted my arm, and I went. I went grudgingly, mind you. I sat there the first day and listened, arms crossed, arrogant, and resistant. It was a large class, so I know the trainer didn't notice, but by the end of the second day, I was converted. He introduced me to what I now call "source-focused thinking" or a source-focused model for dealing with trauma. It took me until Wednesday to hear God saying to me, "Didn't you ask me to show you what to do with this client? Well, this is it!"

After completing the workshop, I introduced the process to this client and many more. I started 2 groups in my outpatient office and a class in my inpatient program. Although later, in 2011, I abandoned that particular model to develop my own spiritually integrated model, I retained the core belief that we must address the root or the source of trauma, that grief is the evidence of healing, not the evidence of disease, and structure is required for successful recovery. Through working with so many clients moving through the grieving process, I learned a lot about what works and what doesn't work.

The main reason I developed the Phase 1 process is that, while the grieving process worked for a high percentage of clients, I still lost some others before they really got started. Those who took these steps first, especially partnering with me for recovery, were able to complete the grieving process successfully. Those who didn't usually dropped out and quit. I partnered with the hospital. They set me up to partner with the trainer. I invested my efforts in learning the model with God's help and my clients partnered with me for healing. Partnering is one of the common factors that make counseling work.

Trauma Myth #4:

I'm sure you've heard this myth said in one way or another, "Time heals all wounds." Researchers assign this quote to Chaucer. It's a line found in one of his stories, A Knights Tale, Palamone and Arcite.[69] They didn't have television or the internet; books were most people's entertainment. Many people read the book, discussed it, and passed the saying around. However, when it comes to trauma, this just isn't true. As Dr. Felliti, one of the main researchers of the ACE study says, "Time doesn't heal, it conceals."[70] The symptoms or survival responses form a mask over your identity, like a Halloween Mask. What people see on the outside, and what you see looking in the mirror are the results of the wound, but may not be the real you; the "you" God created you to be. Removing this mask requires healing at the root level.

Stage 4

Stage 4: I am forming a partnership with at least one other person (counselor or recovery coach) with whom I will move on to Phase Two in order to boldly identify (and finish grieving the sources of) my wounds in a focused and structured manner.

We are moving into the final stage of Phase One, looking toward Phase Two, and finishing our final preparations for moving on to the Reprocessing and Grieving Phase. Remember that reprocessing the traumatic events is the heart of Strategic Trauma and Abuse Recovery©. Phase 1 only serves as preparation for starting and completing the stages of Phase 2. Doing it alone, however, is not only daunting, but also not possible. A very important part of healing is sharing the process with another person with whom you are emotionally connected, someone who can walk with you through this healing in an empathetic manner.

Participation in successful trauma healing requires companionship, courage, and control of your choices. I know we all want to do it alone; especially Americans (my cultural heritage). Sharing the deepest wounds of our hearts leaves us feeling vulnerable. It's embarrassing to share some of the things that were done to us by loved ones in our past. We see it as somehow a reflection of who we were or are, so we want

117

to heal in secret. The human brain is not wired that way. God wired us for connection. Trauma occurred because of expectations in relationship with others, that's part of what made it trauma. Healing takes place through relationship with others. A natural survival response is to isolate yourself to protect you from getting hurt. While this works to some extent, your expectations and need for connections continue. You can read this book and even write out your stories; but without the participation of sharing your stories with someone who cares, who listens and responds appropriately, healing will be limited.

Successful recovery requires courage. Any type of traumatic experience is discouraging. To be discouraged means to have courage taken from you; think of it as a wound much like a physical wound that causes blood loss. It takes courage to face the fact that the trauma occurred to YOU; to consider letting go of survival responses that might be helpful on the one hand, but interfering with your life goals on the other; and to face painful emotions you thought were gone forever. Summon the courage you have left to begin or continue your journey of recovery. You must have some courage left; after all, you are already participating in this class or reading this book!

Successful recovery requires control of your choices. No one can make you recover, no can make you grieve; you have to want it. You get to decide what you want out of your life. If someone else is more invested in your recovery than you are and wants you to read this book or attend the class. Great! Perhaps you will be inspired and make a choice to start the journey to recovery. Nevertheless, it is YOUR choice, not anyone else's. Whatever you decide to do, it's up to you; it's your choice, it's your life. Do with it what YOU want. However, doing nothing is choosing not to heal. You must be pro-active to heal trauma, you must participate in the healing.

I want you to be thinking about transition into the grieving stage. "Forming a partnership with at least one other person"—means a counselor or recovery coach trained in walking with you through the structured grief process (Phase Two) of Strategic Trauma and Abuse Recovery© (S.T.A.R.). "At least"—means that you can do this one-on-one or in a group. Again, I want to emphasize and pound away at the point that you can't do it alone; and models that tell you that you can, well they are just wrong. God made us to be in relationship; God works through others to bring healing. I know you want to heal at home, alone, in private. You want to heal inside your head without actually talking to anyone or telling your story. You want to keep your grief inside and not feel vulnerable. However, does keeping it to yourself make you less vulnerable or more vulnerable? I really think it makes you more vulnerable because it increases your "blind spots".

Wisdom says, "A person standing alone can be attacked and defeated, but two can stand back-to-back and conquer. Three are even better, for a triple-braided cord is not easily broken" (Ecclesiastes 4:2). Galatians 6:2 is the core verse for this class. Paul said, "Bear one another's burdens and fulfill the law of Christ." Paul knew we would have problems. Salvation doesn't take away our past, give us a new brain or a wiped memory. Salvation doesn't put us in a bubble where we aren't affected by life and the world around us. Far from it! It sensitizes us to the pain going on around us. When you experience salvation, the Holy Spirit, the Spirit of Christ, comes to dwell inside of you. He draws hurting people to you, and draws you to hurting people. He makes the contrast between your pain and His peace more definable in an incremental manner. While the philosophies of Buddhism and Stoicism, which are both common in the treatment of psychological disorders, teach detachment from self and the world around you, the Bible teaches love, passion, and caring. It teaches awareness of self and inner healing of your identity. It teaches transformation and sanctification. It also teaches connection with people.

EXPERIENCING EMPATHY

Partnering is difficult because our brains don't really want us to be that vulnerable. Traumatic experiences, especially those from loved ones but also those from strangers, implant shame into our identity. In addition, it doesn't take trauma to cause shame, it only takes awareness of our own imperfection. Shame is a powerful force that not only keeps us hidden away from others, blocks us from admitting the reality of our vulnerability, and leads to blame, but also prevents us from receiving empathy. Lewis B. Smedes, a professor at Fuller Theological Seminary, writes about shame this way, "A vague, undefined heaviness that presses on our spirit, dampens our gratitude for the goodness of life, and slackens the free flow of joy. Shame...seeps into and discolors all our other feelings, primarily about ourselves, but about almost everyone and everything else in our life as well."[71]

The internal experience of shame, no matter how we try to repress it, continues to influence our interactions with people around us. Brené Brown says there are three things shame needs to grow, secrecy, silence, and judgment.[72] As it continues to grow, shame drives defensiveness, oversensitivity to others, and anger. You may not even know why you are so angry all the time, you may not consciously connect it to the shame you carry. In fact, you may appear to others to be arrogant and aloof, uncaring, and unsympathetic to another's difficulty. You may be trying to hide your shame and withdraw emotionally and resist connection with the people who love you, even blaming them for not connecting to you. These tiny signals, sent back and forth between human beings from deep down inside connect us or drive us apart.[73]

Let's clarify the difference between guilt and shame. Guilt is the normal feeling everyone feels when they do something bad. You feel convicted by your conscious and by God's law and you feel guilty. Shame is about who you are as a person, not about your behavior. That's why people feel shame over what was done to them, but guilt over what they did in response. The two become confused in your mind and difficult to separate. Sometimes, shame is easier to feel than guilt because it gives you a false sense of control, something like: "I could have controlled that, stopped it from happening," even when you really couldn't have.

The ultimate answer to personal guilt and shame is salvation through Christ and seeing yourself the way God sees you: forgiven and whole. Empathy and compassion work to conquer shame in your relationships with others as you go through this transformation from the inside out. Empathy is, "the capacity for the understanding, being aware of, being sensitive to, and vicariously experiencing the feelings, thoughts, and experience of another." In other words, you're putting yourself in someone else's place and feeling with them about an experience. Compassion is, "sympathetic consciousness of others' distress together with a desire to alleviate it." In other words, you have the ability to put yourself in their place and you care about their pain enough to want to take it away.

Brené Brown is a research professor at the University of Houston Graduate College of Social Work and TED speaker who has spent the last 12 years researching vulnerability, courage, worthiness, and shame. She has found that, while sympathy drives disconnection, empathy drives connection.[74] She points out four attributes of empathy defined by Theresa Wiseman. These include, 1. Being able to see the world as others see it, 2. To be nonjudgmental, 3. To understand another person's feelings, and 4. To communicate your understanding of that person's feelings.[75] Empathy is a skill, something you have to learn. If you can learn it, you can improve, and in order to improve, you need to practice. Notice it doesn't end with awareness of the other's feelings but also includes the ability to communicate this to the other. A prerequisite to empathy, according to Wiseman, is self-awareness. This means you have to connect to something inside of you that connects with something inside of the other person. You have to be aware of your inner pain, be willing to touch it, and connect to it; you have to be vulnerable in order to experience empathy with other people.

The Bible is full of encouragement for Christians to be compassionate, to be empathetic with others, and to accept empathy. I believe that this is what Paul had in mind when he wrote the end of his letter to the Galatian Christians. In this letter, Paul wrote about the restoring of "sinners". The original word used for restoration in verse 1 is *katartizete* and it means to set into joint[76], much like setting a broken bone or putting an out-of-joint shoulder back in place. Matthew and Mark use the same verb in Matthew 4:21 and Mark 1:19 to mean the mending of fishing nets. This is similar to the concept of emotional and psychological healing through relationship. One Bible commentator says that Paul "calls for spiritual therapy so that a broken member of the body can once again work properly and perform its vital functions for the benefit of the whole body."[77] At the same time in Galatians 6:1, Paul demonstrates compassion for the hurting by using terminology that encourages empathy, not judgment. One way he does this is by writing, "...if someone is trapped in sin..." implying that the sinner has been hunted, captured, and held against his or her will.[78] Once again, God's repeats His design for healing our physical body in His design for psychological and emotional healing.

God demonstrates empathy and compassion continuously. The ultimate expression of empathy because of His compassion was when he literally put himself in our place by sending Jesus to be born as a human baby to experience all the vulnerabilities a baby has, as well as all the temptations a child, adolescent, and an adult has, too. Christ then allowed men to crucify Him, bearing the sin of all humanity for all time, sacrificing Himself in the place of everyone who has ever, or will ever, be born. His empathy with us allows us to empathize with each other. This was not a last ditch effort, either. This was His plan from the beginning.

Jesus demonstrated empathy when He was with Mary before raising Lazarus from the dead. In John 11:33-35 we read, "When Jesus saw her weeping and saw the other people wailing with her, a deep anger welled up within him, and he was deeply troubled. 'Where have you put him?' he asked them. They told him, 'Lord, come and see.' Then Jesus wept." While some might interpret verse 33 to mean Jesus was angry with them for a lack of faith, perhaps Jesus was angry at death itself and angry at how it terrorizes us on Earth.

Then Jesus asked them where Lazarus' body was (vs. 34) and they invited Him to come and see. This triggered weeping on Jesus' part (vs. 35). He didn't wail (*klaio*) like they did, but He wept (*dakyro*); He shed tears. He hadn't come to the tomb yet, so He wasn't weeping over Lazarus; besides, He knew He would be raising Lazarus, so there was no need for Him to weep over Lazarus. It appears that Jesus was showing empathy by putting Himself in the place of Mary, Martha, and their friends; He was sharing in their grief. This is the attitude of empathy you can demonstrate with others and the attitude you want demonstrated with you. Because you know that Jesus was God and man here on Earth and He showed to all humanity who God really is, you can know that God the Father empathizes with you, too; both in your daily experiences and your traumatic losses. In turn, when you show empathy to others, you are demonstrating Jesus to them in a real way.

One final example of Paul encouraging empathy is in his first letter to the Thessalonians. Paul wrote, "Brothers and sisters, we urge you to warn those who are lazy. Encourage those who are timid. Take tender care of those who are weak. Be patient with everyone." One expression of empathy will not make everything better. We have to be patient with ourselves and with each other as we move through the healing process. Ongoing empathy and compassion help to facilitate healing, not "fixing". We designed the structure you will learn for sharing your stories and listening to other survivors' stories specifically to foster and teach you how to both receive empathy and show empathy, while maintaining patience and the right balance between vulnerability and safety.

Healing together can provide comfort, en-courage-ment, and companionship. Some of us really struggle to ask for help or allow someone to help us. We want comfort, but think we have to give it to ourselves, forgetting that we aren't alone. Being alone is common for trauma survivors because of the losses of trust and safety. It's hard to trust people not to judge you when you share your pain with them, and not to betray you by disclosing your secrets to others. Knowing who you can trust is important because the truth is, some people might judge and others might betray.

PARTNERING IS GOD'S IDEA

Partnering for healing isn't a new idea, nor is it original. In Genesis 2, we read, "18 Then the Lord God said, "It is not good for the man to be alone. I will make a helper who is just right for him." When Jesus was on Earth, He sent the disciples out in pairs, not alone. Jesus partnered with His closest friends, Peter, James, and John, but also with the rest of His 12 disciples.

One example of successful partnering for healing is shared by Dr. Luke in Luke 5:17-25. Jesus was in a house, possibly thought to be His house by some Bible scholars, teaching. People had packed in to house, shoulder to shoulder. Definitely not to current fire-code standards! Many of the people there were Pharisees and teachers of religious law who were really only there to try to argue with Jesus and disprove His claims. These people were taking up so much space, that no one else could get in. A group of friends, "some men," the text reads, had heard about Jesus and wanted to get their paralyzed friend in front of him, hoping for healing. I have heard pastors joke that they must have been teenagers, because only teenagers would be so bold as to climb up on the roof and tear it apart to get to Jesus. That is what they did. They put their paralyzed friend on a mat or bed of some kind, then, seeing the place was just too full to get in and get to Jesus, they decided the best thing to do was to climb up onto the roof, hoisting their paralyzed friend—who had to be terrified—up on to the roof with them.

In those days, they used thatched roofing, probably mud and grass mixed together and dried into tiles. Obviously, the roof was strong enough to hold them, but the people inside had to know that someone was climbing on the roof. They had to wonder, "*What is going on up there?*" Eventually, they were able to pull away enough tiles to lower their friend down on ropes to the ground right in front of Jesus. That took some skill, some massive courage, and divine guidance. In vs 20, Luke points out that Jesus saw their faith. Their faith was active, not passive. They KNEW Jesus could heal their friend. Here, we have another clue that they may have been teenagers because Jesus looked at the man and said, "Young man, your sins are forgiven."

This was a bold move by Jesus, since He knew the Pharisees and teachers of the law were there trying to find fault with Him. By saying this, He was proclaiming that He was God. They, of course, noticed it, and Jesus knew what they were thinking. Therefore, he followed it up with a challenge. Which one is harder to say, your sins are forgiven (we can't see that or prove it) or you are healed from paralysis—something you can see right now? Obviously, it's harder to say you are healed because the proof will be in the man's behavior. Making his point, the man got up and walked! The partnering of these men with their paralyzed, helpless, and hopeless friend had paid off! Jesus response was to heal him from the inside out, proving He was God.

Another story about partnering to win comes from the Old Testament, 1 Samuel 14. Saul was king at the time and he had his 600 elite fighting men set up in Geba near the Philistine army. One of these elite fighting men was his own son, Jonathan. Evidently, they had been camped there a while and Jonathan was getting antsy. One day, Jonathan told the soldier who carried his weapons that he wanted to attack the Philistine camp on the other side of the valley. They slipped out of the Israelite camp without anyone knowing it. Jonathan didn't even tell his father he was leaving. As they were walking to the Philistine camp, Jonathan shared his vision with the soldier. Evidently, they were close and Jonathan really believed he could trust this man. His vision was to go get something started and trust that God could use the two of them to win the entire battle against the godless Philistines. This brave soldier, whose name the writer never mentions, pledged his faithfulness and trust to both Jonathan and God saying he would do whatever Jonathan asked him to do. What a powerful partnership!

They had to climb down into a valley and cross over to the hill on which the other army was camped. Jonathan had asked God to give them a sign as to whether or not He wanted them to continue. If the other army saw them at the bottom of the hill, and the other soldiers came down, they'd fight down at the bottom of the hill. However, if the soldiers invited them up to the top of the hill that would be God's sign that He wanted them to continue and would help them win the battle. When they got there, the soldiers invited them up to fight and Jonathan led the way up the hill with confidence knowing God was going to let them win.

In true partnership fashion, they stood back to back and fought the entire Philistine encampment. The passage reads, "Before they had gone a hundred feet, they had killed about twenty Philistines" (vs 14). This panicked the whole camp and, to add to it, God partnered with them too. God sent an earthquake right at that moment, terrifying the Philistines! At a distance and from higher up, King Saul saw this. He described the chaos in the camp "like melted wax" (vs 16). He decided to get his 598 men over there, but "by this time the Philistines were so confused that they were killing each other" (vs 20). By the time he got there, some of the hired soldiers who weren't Philistines had switched sides and started fighting for Israel's side. There were also many Israelites hiding in the hills who had been too afraid to come out but, because of the movement that Jonathan and his weapon carrier had started, they joined the fight too. Using this partnership, God helped Israel to win the battle against the Philistines that day.

Forming a partnership with someone you trust, someone who is trustworthy, and knows what they are doing *can start an entire movement.* This will not just be victory and healing for you alone, but for those around you, too. The armor bearer bravely partnered with Jonathan and with God to defeat the entire camp. When they did their part, God did His. They did what they could do, and God did something they could have never done. The paralyzed man partnered with his friends, who partnered with each other to get him to Jesus. They cared more about their friend's life and salvation than they did their own reputation. Jesus responded by healing him inside—forgiving his sins—and outside.

You might be reading this book as a part of an organized ministry who can refer you to a local counselor or recovery coach trained in the S.T.A.R. method, who can walk with you through Phase 2. You may even have a Phase 2 trauma group available to join. However, what do you do if you are reading this on your own with none of those resources available? First, you can check out our website at www. TraumaEducation.com to find someone near you or explore some distance options. A trained person who is trustworthy, ethical, someone you can connect with, and someone who can really empathize with you is vital.

Vulnerability is the key to healing, but if you want to share your trauma with a friend, there are some friends you probably shouldn't share with. Brené Brown points out that these include:

1. Friends who overreact and feel your pain for you.

2. Friends who only know how to express sympathy and not empathy, they kind of look down on you with, "That's awful. I wouldn't want to have your life!"

3. Friends who put you on a pedestal or idolize you and who will be shattered and disappointed in your "failure" to be perfect.

4. Friends who are uncomfortable with being vulnerable themselves.

5. Friends who minimize because they are so uncomfortable and say things like, "It isn't that bad."

6. Friends who want to "one-up" you with something like, "You think that's bad, wait to you hear what happened to me!"[79] Finally, if you are a Christian, don't choose a friend who doesn't understand or believe that God heals trauma. If your friend is a Christian, make sure they can also fit the previous criteria and empathize with your pain.

FEEDING YOUR FAITH BY JOINING THE CONVERSATION

I've suggested several ways to "feed your faith" in the last several chapters. They include praying, reading the Bible, worshipping, and listening to Christian music of any genre. In this chapter, I want to suggest listening to other, more faith-filled Christians talk about God and *joining* in the conversation. This can be very challenging for trauma survivors who may tend to feel ashamed, lack confidence, and don't know who to trust. Perhaps you are still learning what the Bible is all about, or have come from a religion that taught you to just think about it, but don't talk about it. Unfortunately, many denominations and religious organizations have allowed the four unspoken rules of dysfunctional homes to creep into their midst. They may silently teach, "Don't talk, don't trust, don't feel, and/or don't think for yourself." Remember, these are NOT God's rules!

God wants us to talk; talk to Him and talk to others both believers and non-believers. Jesus talked to everyone, people who agreed with Him and people who didn't. God kept talking to Moses even when Moses argued with Him. Moses swayed God with his argument not to kill all of the Israelites in the desert and raise up a new people from him (Exodus 32:11-14). Take this opportunity to find a group of Christian believers that you can trust (use the guidelines mentioned previously and in the next chapter) and listen to them, then ask questions. While many Christians will entertain difficult questions, some won't. If you only get trite answers, move on to someone else. You can also listen to sermons online, to podcasts, and to various preachers, both male and female, on YouTube.com. However, it is very important to find a place you can *ask questions*, you can *discuss*, you can *make comments*, and you can *challenge* your old beliefs that may or may not be accurate. Join the conversation and continue to feed your faith in God!

In the next and final chapter of this book, we will overview what Phase 2 looks like as you continue your journey of healing from trauma.

Chapter 6 Summary

1. Partnering with a trusted counselor or recovery coach is one of the common factors that makes counseling work.

2. Trauma myth #4, "Time heals all wounds" is a quote from a fairy tale. When it comes to trauma, time does not heal, it conceals.

3. Stage 4 is the final stage of Phase One and reads, "I am forming a partnership with at least one other person (counselor or recovery coach) with whom I will move on to Phase Two in order to boldly identify (and finish grieving the sources of) my wounds in a focused and structured manner.

4. Participation in successful trauma healing requires companionship, courage, and control of your choices.

5. Everyone wants to heal at home, alone, and in private, but trauma healing doesn't work that way. You can't do it alone and models that tell you that you can are just wrong. God created us to be in relationship; God works through others to bring about emotional healing.

6. Shame is a powerful force that keeps us hidden away from others, blocks us from admitting the reality of our vulnerability, leads to blame, and prevents us from receiving empathy.

7. Guilt and shame become confused in our mind and difficult to separate. Sometimes, shame is easier to feel than guilt because it gives you a false sense of control. Like, "I could have controlled that, and stopped it from happening," when you really couldn't have.

8. Empathy and compassion work to conquer shame in your re-

lationships with others as you go through this transformation from the inside out.

9. Empathy is a skill and can be taught and practiced. Self-awareness is a prerequisite for empathy.

10. God demonstrates compassion and empathy continuously. Jesus demonstrated empathy while on Earth. Paul encouraged empathy.

11. Healing together can provide comfort, en-courage-ment, and companionship. One expression of empathy will not make everything better. We have to be patient with ourselves and with each other as we move through the healing process.

12. Forming a partnership with someone you trust, someone who is trustworthy, and knows what they are doing can start an entire movement—not only victory and healing for you, but for those around you, too.

13. Vulnerability is the key to healing and, but if you want to share your trauma with a friend, there are some friends you probably shouldn't share with.

14. Another way to feed your faith is to listen to other, more faith-filled Christians talk about God and *join* in the conversation.

CHAPTER 7:
MOVING FROM
FAITH TO HOPE

"Plans succeed through good counsel; don't go to war without wise advice."

Proverbs 20:18-19

When I was growing up, my family moved a LOT. I was born in Chico, CA and started kindergarten there. My dad got a great new job and, after only a few weeks in school in Chico, we moved to Santa Clara. As the law required, my parents put me in school right away. Unfortunately, the apartment we moved into was disgusting, so after about two weeks, we moved to San Jose into The Garden of Eden apartments. I started my third kindergarten class. When I started first grade the next year, while we were still living in the same place, I started a new school. By then I had developed a serious anxiety disorder. Every morning before school, I was sick. I had diarrhea and sometimes vomiting. I hated school, I was miserable, and fast on my way to having an ulcer.

There were other things that added to my anxiety; like a car accident that gave me a concussion when I was 5 or 6; my teenage cousins moving in when the state removed them from their parent's home; my youngest brother being born 3 months pre-mature with the cord wrapped around his neck; and my mom losing her last baby near full-term. However, mostly, it was the moving that got me overly anxious at that time. When I finished second grade, we moved into a house in Santa Clara and I started a new school. Half-way through fourth grade, we moved to Salinas, CA where I completed fourth and fifth grade. For sixth grade, we moved back to San Jose. For seventh grade, we moved to Hayward, CA. This was the closest we had lived to San Francisco and the school we attended was tough, with gangs and all. Therefore, for eighth grade, though we lived in the same place, my parents moved us to a private Christian school. Toward the end of eighth grade, with only a couple of months to go, we moved to Piper, KS. I finished eighth grade and then started high school, at another school of course. I finished tenth grade there, and we promptly moved to Lawrenceville, GA where I finished 11th and 12th grades. Before I was done, I had attended 11 different schools!

While frequent moving may not fit into most definitions of what could be considered "trauma", because it's not life threatening, it was for me and is for many people. Trauma, regardless of the actual type of event, creates a toxic level of stress. Raising the level of stress to the toxic range is part of what makes an event traumatic. That doesn't mean it has to be a life-threatening event. I have focused a lot on childhood trauma in this book, but adult trauma has many of the same affects, just not on young brain architecture. Research has demonstrated that adults affected by non-life-threatening events can experience significant Post-Traumatic Stress Disorder-like symptoms. For example, following an outbreak of foot and mouth disease among livestock in the Netherlands in 2001, nearly 50% of the farmers who were required to put livestock down demonstrated symptoms of post-traumatic stress at such significant levels they required professional help.[80]

In other studies, events considered everyday life events, including relationship discord, non-sudden death of a loved one, chronic illness, and problems with work or school, caused more PTSD symptoms in adults than events considered life threatening such as accidents or disasters.[81] This research indicated the need to redefine trauma, and to consider assessing and treating individuals affected by everyday life events, rather than only looking at events considered life threatening. As you can see, toxic levels of stress take a toll on your mind, brain, and body regardless of your age or level of maturity. Continuing on to the Reprocessing and Grieving phase, in spite of your fear and anxiety, is the path to healing.

TRAUMA MYTH #5

As you move toward phase two, you are probably feeling a little anxious. Trauma myth #5 grows out of that fear. It goes something like this, "Talking about the details of past trauma just re-traumatizes a person. You should never ask (tell) people about the details." As a new counselor, I attended a workshop presented by the Georgia Counsel on Child abuse. The topic was on working with adult survivors of sexual abuse. In that class, they told us that we should NOT ask survivors to share their stories because that would "re-traumatize" them. This myth has continued even up until today. Much of it is because of caregivers' fears of hearing the story and not knowing what to do with it after it's shared. Caregivers, like counselors, social workers, marriage and family therapists, pastoral counselors, addiction counselors, etc., continue to express this fear that if I "open them up, I have to put them back together." This is so far from the truth! If you have survived the actual event, you can certainly survive remembering, sharing, and grieving over the past. Eventually, at the right time, you have to share the details of your story. You don't have to share the details with everyone, but with the counselor who will empathize, demonstrate compassion, listen, and be interested in the story.

The most common mistake people make is not sharing the details of their story. The second most common mistake is sharing it too soon or with the wrong people.[82] The healing process is in sharing your story in an emotionally connected relationship, not from a stage, or in a book, but with someone who cares, who has a plan, and who can lead you through the process of healing. It may be tempting to start telling your story to everyone who will listen, but this may not be wise. Sharing your pain with an insensitive person can lead to more pain and a strong desire not to share again with anyone.

The thing about this particular myth, which I dislike the most, is that it denies your God-given resilience. In stage one we talked about accepting powerlessness, and the difference between being powerless and being helpless. You are definitely powerless, but you are not helpless because God created you to be resilient! Let's revisit the prophecy of Isaiah 40:6 where God told him to remind the people that "All flesh is as frail as grass" While grass is weak, it is also resilient. The definition of resilience is "an ability to recover from or adjust easily to misfortune or change"[83] or "the capability of a strained body to recover its size and shape after deformation caused especially by compressive stress."[84] God designed humans to be resilient. While the survival responses developed because of trauma may have negative side effects, they actually work. You are a survivor! You have survived incredible pain, just as I have. While my life is not perfect by any means, I am enjoying ongoing healing and God is continually giving me more peace and continually transforming me into His image. He is doing the same thing for you, as you let Him. Believe in the resilience God has given you. Have faith in Him that as you move on to the work of writing and reprocessing that He will continue to restore you.

WHAT TO EXPECT IN PHASE TWO: USING STRATEGIC STRUCTURE

We strategically designed Phase 1 to move you through healing in an incremental fashion while feeding your faith in God. We also designed Phase 2 using a strategy. To be "strategic" means to have a plan, to be calculating, intentional, and deliberate. In fact, Phase 2 requires more structure since we are exposing more of the wound. While you may complete Phase 1 in a classroom, you will complete Phase 2 in either individual counseling or in a structured group of six to eight like-minded people with a trained counselor or S.T.A.R. Coach. Most people leading the Phase 2 structure will be specifically educated and trained in professional counseling, social work, addiction counseling, or marriage and family therapy. They will probably also charge a fee for their services, even if your Phase 1 facilitator did not.

Paying a fee for counseling is important to consider because, sometimes, you get what you pay for. The counselor working with you will be investing his or her time, energy and passion for imparting the process of healing to you; and, as Paul wrote in 1 Timothy 5: 17-18,

"Elders who do their work well should be respected and paid well, [e] especially those who work hard at both preaching and teaching. 18 For the Scripture says, 'You must not muzzle an ox to keep it from eating as it treads out the grain.' And in another place, 'Those who work deserve their pay!'" The science and art of Christian-integrated professional counseling is a calling. It's a ministry and the way by which counselors make a living. Counseling is a spiritual gift and practice ordained by God. In fact, some consider it the most practical application of pastoral care or "pastoring." Therefore, don't let paying for the services of a professional, Biblically-based Christian counselor keep you from moving forward. You probably invest in many other things to improve your outside like clothes, nails, haircuts, makeup, and other hobby items. Make investing in your "inside" a priority and move ahead in healing.

Once you start in Phase 2, your counselor will teach you how to use structure in your writing, and structure in your processing. The complete details are included in the next book and provided by your trained counselor. They will have all of the handouts you need and be able to teach you what to do every step of the way. You never have to wander around trying to figure out what to do next.

We have laid the path out for you following the six stages of Phase 2:

1. I am courageously choosing to tell my story using structure and detail to my counselor/recovery coach, and, when possible, my fellow group members.

2. I am identifying the beliefs that have grown out of the hurtful events, beliefs about me, life, others, and God (spirituality, religion, or church) along with my initial responses.

3. I am humbly identifying and admitting to myself and my partner or group, my own survival responses even when they contradict my own expectations of myself.

4. I am embracing and grieving all of the losses I experienced with this source of trauma; those the offender caused me, and those caused by my own survival responses.

5. After completing this thorough inventory of my experiences,

contradicted expectations, losses, survival behaviors and the losses these caused me, I humbly and courageously choose forgiveness; forgiving my perpetrator for robbing me and forgiving myself (as I have been forgiven) for my responses.

6. I understand that healing is an ongoing process from the inside out, and I humbly acknowledge where I've come from and those who have contributed to my healing and will make a spiritual or personal marker to represent where I have traveled on my path of healing with this source of trauma.

You will work through these stages in order, applying them to one source of trauma at a time before starting on another source. A "source" of trauma is usually a person. Most of our expectations in life are about relationships and people; therefore, most contradictions to our expectations come through people. Some examples include 1. A father who was physically abusive; 2. A mother who was absent; 3. A parent who was an addict; 4. An uncle who was sexually abusive; and 5. A husband/wife having an extra-marital affair. However, trauma could also be a non-person related event. Some examples include: 1. A hurricane, 2. A car accident; 3. A crime perpetrated by a stranger, like robbery or rape.

After identifying all of your sources of trauma with your counselor's help, and using the Simple Trauma Source Assessment©, your counselor will you decide which one you should start with. Some people may have only one identifiable source; others may have two, three, or even 10. You will make this decision together with your counseling in a collaborative fashion, within some guidelines. Usually, you should start with the most pressing source of trauma. Most pressing means the one that is occupying your conscious thoughts the most; this is usually the most recently occurring source, but could be an early childhood source or previously experienced adult source. Your counselor will work with you to help you decide where to start. Once identified, I typically have people arrange or number a list in chronologically descending order. Most recent is #1, while the source that happened the earliest in life is last.

ADDICTION AS A SOURCE OF TRAUMA

It's important to distinguish between trauma sources and survival responses. Sometimes you might be confused about where to start. The only survival response that we would write about is addiction. Substance use starts out as a survival response, but for some people, it grows into an addiction. If you are currently, or have recently been, in treatment for substance abuse, have received a diagnosis of substance use disorder, or have been in self-help groups like Alcoholics Anonymous° or Narcotics Anonymous° in order to get sober, you should probably start by writing about your addiction, as a source of trauma. This may be unusual, but is quite effective.

No one plans or even thinks they will become an addict. The definition of addiction is vague and hard to define. Some people who have been using drugs or alcohol daily can suddenly stop and never go back to using. However, addiction leaves a path of destruction in its wake. I think of it like a date-rapist. You go out on a date with someone you think is safe and the next thing you know they are making you do things you would have never otherwise done. Even after a person gets sober, the impact of the trauma of the addiction is still there. Some people say, "dry-drunk" or "addictive personality". Addicts experience the same stages listed in the Trauma Survivor Blueprint©, the same contradictions and the same losses. Processing through the trauma of addiction is as important as processing through childhood sexual abuse. Usually, I start with the addiction first. If this is you, you will be in a special addicts-in-recovery-only group. Be sure and let your counselor know if this is one of your sources of trauma along with all of the other sources.

AVOIDING THE "ROUND-ROBIN DEFENSE"

It is important to stick to it once you chose your source of trauma and begin the writing and reading process. It is usually not beneficial to deter from this source. Switching sources plays into the natural defense mechanism of the brain: the Round-Robin Defense©.

The Round-Robin Defense© is a common way for your brain to avoid the pain of grief by moving from one source of trauma to another, dipping your toe in the pain of grief and withdrawing to go to another source. While you might feel a little relief, you never really accomplish healing the wound. It is your counselor's job to help you stay focused using the structure and the safe relationship established in the counseling sessions. In order to combat the Round-Robin Defense©, you should, 1. Start with the most recent source that has the most recent impact on your life. 2. Start with the source that is at the top of your brain and easiest to access. Think of your brain like a Pez˙ dispenser. When you pull back the top of the Pez˙, there is one candy on top. You have to pull that one out to get to the next. Each person's brain has their own way of organizing different sources of trauma. You should work with your counselor to decide how yours is organized. 3. Once you start, don't switch. If another source becomes pressing and is most recent, perhaps you chose the wrong source to start with and need to switch. 4. If you and your counselor agree to switch, only switch once. Complete the new source before moving to the next. 5. Remind yourself that: Switching will result in never completing any sources. Switching is a way that the brain uses to avoid grief; it's a form of bargaining. You will give each source of trauma its own individual focus in the order that best works for you.

INDIVIDUAL OR GROUP COUNSELING

Once you have decided to get started in Phase 2, the next decision you have to make is whether you want to complete it in individual counseling, just you and a counselor, or in a group process. The counselor will start in individual, just to get to know you a little, do the normal evaluations, make sure you understand what's expected and practice the structured writing and reading with you. You may continue the entire six-stage process of Phase 2 with your individual counselor, but I think you will be missing out if you do. While you have more privacy and flexibility with individual sessions, you are missing the total burden-bearer experience. Working together in a group is difficult at first, you have to get to know each other and build some trust. Once you do, having someone who is walking the path with you is such a blessing and a rich experience.

While there is some research on the effectiveness of group therapy vs individual therapy, I'm going to call on my own experience here. The S.T.A.R. process works whether you do it alone with a counselor, or with a counselor and 6-7 other people also working through their own S.T.A.R. process. The advantages of group include: creating a new support system, hearing feedback from someone who has a similar source of trauma, mutual sharing rather than one-way sharing, and experiencing synergy—the energy and drive that is built only by working side-by-side through difficult tasks. It's also motivational. Once you really commit to the group, you are motivated to be there with people who are excited to see you and depend on you being there to grieve with them.

SNOWBALLING YOUR HOPE

The focus in Phase 1 has been using faith to find safety and stability while you prepare to move into Phase 2. The focus of Phase 2 will be building your hope as you re-process traumatic events and grieve your contradictions and losses. I defined faith in chapter 2 as the firm or confident belief in something that has not yet been proven. We looked at Hebrews 11:1, "Faith is the confidence that what we hope for will actually happen; it gives us assurance about things we cannot see." We discussed the fact that everyone has faith in something and that faith is always a choice. Faith sometimes is synonymous with trust. To have faith in someone is to trust him or her.

Hope is a little different from faith. Hope is a "desire with expectation of obtainment." While faith is a confident belief, hope moves forward into expectation of having your desire fulfilled. Think of standing and looking across a chasm, and on the other side is the healing that you want. Faith means I believe I'm going to get that, even though there is this giant chasm between us. Hope is moving toward the chasm, taking that first step and expecting that now you will get it. There is a scene in "Indiana Jones: The Last Crusade" where Indy has to get across a chasm to get to the hiding place of the Cup of Christ. Nothing appears until he takes a leap of faith. When the pathway appears, he keeps moving because his hope that the Cup of Christ is on the other side increases. Though he's hesitant at first, he moves across it eagerly anticipating getting to the other side.[85] This is what your next step involves. A leap of faith! When you take that leap, you will begin to "snowball" your hope for healing and will eagerly move through the stages toward complete healing.

Hope is an important virtue and a lot of research exists on the benefits of feeling hope. One research study showed that hope is the most powerful predictor of well-being.[86] Another study showed that HIV/AIDS and cancer patients who score high on hope have less distress, and less fear of dying.[87] Marital counseling interventions that mix hope and forgiveness decrease irrational marital beliefs among couples.[88] Research on hope shows that generally a positive, hopeful mindset leads to successful coping and good health, while hopelessness and despair leads to illness and disability.[89] The level of hope a person has affects their attitudes about life. In addition, hope is negatively associated with depression and positively associated with life satisfaction.[90]

Hope and despair are important in change.[91] Despair has to occur for us to appreciate hope. Despair without hope is endless and leads to death. Paul wrote in 1 Thessalonians 4: 13, "And now, dear brothers and sisters, we want you to know what will happen to the believers who have died so you will not grieve like people who have no hope." He didn't say we wouldn't grieve, and wouldn't feel despair, but that we could have hope because of the resurrection of the dead. However, we can also have hope because of the resurrection of the oppressed, of the downtrodden, and of the traumatized. Demoralization is truly at the root of many mental health problems, and hope in Christ can bring much relief and healing.

Fear crowds out hope. Fear takes over the brain circuitry, dominating the processing of information and life experiences. Think of it as a bully in your own brain. Traumatic experiences rob us of hope and leave behind a fear of reliving and remembering the experience. Hopelessness, despair, anguish and depression set in when the cycle of grief is stuck. Facing your memories, feelings, and the reality of those experiences in an intentional and structured manner with support and empathy from others increasingly restores your hope. Not immediately, but like a snowball. To make a giant snowball fit for a good-sized snowman you start with just a fist-full of snow. Then you pack more onto that, then more and more and more. Soon you can roll the large ball around and more snow will stick to it, increasing its size. It's gradual, but intentional, and you must have a strategy to keep it from falling apart.

TRAUMA MYTH #6:

This is the final myth we will address in this book and it goes something like this, "Positive thinking will overcome trauma." As I already mentioned, positive thinking is associated with great health benefits. It is a great way to live your life and is the basis for many approaches to dealing with symptoms like depression, anxiety, and personality disorders. However, denying the reality of real trauma and loss leaves room for fear in your life and continues to rob you of hope. In cases like this, positive thinking works to keep you distracted on the future or something outside of you rather than dealing with the reality of your own internally stored pain and loss. At the root of this false belief is also stoic philosophy, which teaches that negative feelings are beneath intelligent and wise people. Unfortunately, you can't selectively numb your emotions; it's all or none.

Positive thinking approaches assert that, if you change your thoughts, you can change your beliefs, and change your life. While this works on some things, when it comes to trauma, it's not always that simple. For one thing, you may not really know what your thoughts and beliefs are. Basic thoughts and beliefs are formed early in life and because of the nature of the brain, we aren't consciously aware of all of our beliefs all of the time. When we learn something new, we form a set of beliefs and these beliefs help us navigate our world. These beliefs come together and form "schemas" or maps of our world, which help us navigate relationships, social situations, scary experiences, and all other parts of our lives. Schemas are like filters through which we see and experience everything around us. They can distort our views of the world and of ourselves.

Changing beliefs that are rooted in survival takes more than will power, and more than practice, more than memorizing or thinking positively. It takes getting to the root of the belief. Tracing a current thought all the way back to its originating point can be very tedious and difficult, if not impossible, especially since your brain will be working against you, blocking out memories of trauma, avoiding the connections because of the pain associated with those memories.

By going straight to the root first, you can take an approach that goes from the originating event to the current thought. Research shows that trauma is at the root of a lot of current pain and survival responses or symptoms, as you've learned in previous chapters. Phase Two has this bottom-up approach all laid out for you in a structured and strategic manner. You start in stage one by writing about the event and identifying its associated contradictions and losses. Then, in stage two, you identify your interpretations of each event, because these interpretations are what have developed into your thoughts and beliefs. In this stage, you also identify the survival responses you developed in response to those beliefs, and in stage three, you connect how those original beliefs and survival responses have morphed into current beliefs and survival responses. You get to make the choice as to whether you will keep using them, or change them. Therefore, it's not that you aren't changing your "stinkin' thinkin'", it's just that you are starting at the root and following a bottom up approach rather than working from the top down.

Adding to the structure of the writing process is the structure of the reading and group responding. This is not your average free-for-all group counseling where people get to say whatever comes to their mind. I led that type of group for years and found it lacking. While it might work for group discussions, it doesn't work when you are expected to share deeply personal experiences and expose horrific wounds. People say hurtful things, turn the focus onto themselves, dominate the group, and generally can't seem to do what needs to be done, which is empathize and focus. We designed the structure to help you, your counselor or coach, and your fellow group members remain focused, safe, and to facilitate empathetic responses to each other's pain.

As you step out on the ledge, as you write and read your first stories, you will probably be miserable and you will grieve. It's also possible that you will be in shock and not have a lot of emotion, to start with. It all depends on where you are stuck in the grief cycle. One client of mine was extremely eager to get started and she wrote 41 stories about her ex-husband over one weekend! I don't recommend that, by the way. She started her reading process and, while several other people in the group cried, she didn't cry at all. She asked me, "Denice, when will I start crying? I feel sad, but just a little." I reassured her that shock was normal and that eventually, her brain would move forward in the grief cycle (healing cycle) and that she would begin to cry. It took a number of weeks, but finally she started crying. Then she asked, "When will I stop?!" Grief is individual and, while there are similarities, no one's expression or length of grief is the same.

As you grieve and go back, write more, read and grieve more, your brain is learning something very important. "I am going to survive. I am resilient!" Eventually, you are going to feel relief, comforted, and a sense of increasing distance from the traumatic experiences. This process builds hope; hope that you can actually put it behind you, hope that you are not alone, and hope that you can really heal. Hope "snowballs" as you continue to move forward and this motivates you to want to do it again!

FEEDING YOUR FAITH BY WATCHING FOR "GOD SIGHTINGS"

We have discussed Simple prayer, Bible reading, using your imagination in worship, and listening to Christian music as ways of feeding your faith. Finally, I'd like to suggest that you watch for "God sightings." I usually pray for a client at the end of the counseling session, if they are okay with that sort of thing. Frequently, I pray, "God show [this person] one thing this week that is special to them. One thing that shows them that YOU are paying attention to them." Then I ask the person to watch for God to show-up in their life. People have come back with amazing anecdotes of little things that God has done; things that were too specific to be coincidental, and that would only mean something to them. This isn't testing God or "throwing out a fleece" to say, "God are you paying attention?" It's about KNOWING that God IS paying attention, IS doing special things, and you are being intentional in anticipating and observing these things.

CONCLUSION

Look back over the chapters and think about what God has shown you through this book. Write them down. Look around in your life and see where God is showing up. Did He provide you with more faith? Does He seem bigger to you than He did when you started reading this book? Has He brought any fellow travelers in recovery to connect with you? What special thing has He done for you this week? Continue to feed your faith in God as you move forward in healing.

Now it's time for you to make a decision. Ask yourself, *Am I ready to move on to Phase 2: Reprocessing and Grieving or do I want to revisit ways of feeding my faith?* Please revisit these stages and these chapters as often as you would like. You can visit my website at www. TraumaEducation.com to check for new books, workbooks, classes and more. I pray healing and blessing on you as you continue your journey to recovery using Strategic Trauma and Abuse Recovery©! It is truly a privilege to get to minister to you through this curriculum. Remember, God is the source of ALL healing, no matter how miraculous or how mundane, and He WANTS to heal YOU!

Chapter 7 Summary

1. Trauma, regardless of the actual type of event, creates a toxic level of stress. Raising the level of stress to the toxic range is part of what makes an event traumatic. That doesn't mean it has to be a life-threatening event.

2. Adult experiences of what other models consider everyday life-events, for example relationship discord, non-sudden death of a loved one, chronic illness, and problems with work or school, were found to generate more PTSD symptoms in adults than events considered life threatening such as accidents or disasters.

3. Trauma myth #5 grows out of fear. It goes something like this, "Talking about the details of past trauma just re-traumatizes a person. You should never ask (tell) people about the details."

4. The most common mistake people make is not sharing the details of their story. The second most common mistake is sharing it too soon or with the wrong people.

5. Trauma myth #5 denies your God-given resilience. Believe in the resilience God has given you. Have faith in Him that as you move on to the work of writing and reprocessing that He will continue to restore you.

6. Just like Phase 1 has been strategically arranged to move you through healing in an incremental fashion while feeding your faith in God (Higher Power if you choose), Phase 2 is also designed using a strategic structure.

7. Phase 2 will probably require some type of payment to a professionally trained counselor.

8. Once you start in Phase 2, your counselor will teach you how to use structure in your writing, and structure in your processing.

9. You will work on one source of trauma at a time. A "source" of trauma is usually a person, but can also be an event like a car accident.

10. Substance use is a survival response to trauma, but S.T.A.R also treats addiction as a *source* of trauma.

11. The structure of Phase 2 helps you to avoid the Round-Robin Defense©.

12. Once you have decided to get started in Phase 2, the next decision you have to make is whether you want to complete it in individual counseling, just you and a counselor, or in a group process.

13. The focus of Phase 2 will be building your hope as you re-process traumatic events and grieve your contradictions and losses.

14. Hope is a "desire with expectation of obtainment." While faith is a confident belief, hope moves forward into expectation of having your desire fulfilled.

15. Hope is an important virtue and a lot of research exists on the benefits of feeling hope.

16. Fear crowds out hope. Fear takes over the brain circuitry, dominating the processing of information and life experiences.

17. Trauma myth #6 is the final myth we will address in this book and it goes something like this, "Positive thinking will overcome trauma."

18. Changing beliefs that are rooted in survival takes more than will power, more than practice, and more than memorizing or thinking positively.

19. In the S.T.A.R. model, it's not that you aren't changing your "stinkin' thinkin'", it's just that you are starting at the root and eliminating it there.

20. We designed the group structure to help you, your counselor or coach, and your fellow group members to remain focused, safe, and to facilitate empathetic responses to each other's pain.

21. As you grieve and go back, write more, read and grieve more, your brain is learning something very important. "I am going to survive. I am resilient!"

22. You can feed your faith by watching for "God sightings."

23. Now it's time for you to make a decision. Am I ready to move on to Phase 2: Reprocessing and Grieving or do I want to revisit ways of feeding my faith? What will *you* decide? Looking for help deciding? Speak to a trained counselor, you class leader, or visit www.TraumaEducation.com

ENDNOTES

Introduction

1 New World Encyclopedia. Retrieved from http://www.newworldencyclopedia.org/entry/Johannes_Kepler

2 Mathison, K. (2012). All Truth is God's Truth — A Reformed Approach to Science and Scripture.

3 Gaeblin, F. (1968). The pattern of God's truth. Chicago, IL. Moody Press.

4 Saunders, S. M., Miller, M. L, and Bright, M. M. (2010). Spiritually conscious psychological care. Professional Psychology: Research and Practice. Vol 41, No. 5, 355-362. American Psychological Association

5 Blake, J. (2012). Two preaching giants and the 'betrayal' that tore them apart. http://www.cnn.com/2012/11/17/us/andy-stanley/index.html

6 Eswine, Z. (2014). Spurgeon's Sorrows: Realistic Hope for Those who Suffer from Depression. Christian Focus Publications.

7 Smith, S. (2015). 'Beloved' Pastor and Seminary Professor Commits Suicide After Being Exposed in Ashley Madison Hack. Retrieved from: http://www.christianpost.com/news/beloved-pastor-and-seminary-professor-commits-suicide-after-being-exposed-in-ashley-madison-hack-144920/#9fLDtEWBB0XbCllG.99

8 Wright, B. (2010) Christians are hate-filled hypocrites...And other Lies you've been told: A sociologist shatters myths from the secular and Christian media. Bethany House Publishers

9 Nissinen, M. (2004). Homoeroticism in the Biblical World: A Historical Perspective. Fortress Press.

10 United Nations Office on Drugs and Crime. (2015). http://www.unodc.org/unodc/en/human-trafficking/what-is-human-trafficking.html?ref=menuside

Chapter 1: Uncovering Hidden Wounds

11 WebMd at http://www.webmd.com/skin-problems-and-treatments/guide/leprosy-symptoms-treatments-history

12 Yancy, P., and Brand, P. (1997). The Gift of Pain. Zondervan.

13 Felitti, V. Ontario lecture?

14 *Encyclopedia of Violence,* 2008

15 Lewis, C. S. (1940). The problem of pain. New York, NY: HarperCollins.

16 TIP 57, Trauma-Informed Care in Behavioral Health Services. (2014). Substance Abuse and Mental Health Services Administration.

17 Why Trauma Matters in Primary Care. (2015). the National Council for Behavioral Health. Retrieved from http://www.thenationalcouncil.org/wp-content/uploads/2013/10/Trauma_matters_infographic.png

18 The Still Face Experiment. www.youtube.com/watch?v=apzXGEbZht0

19 Felitti, V. J., Anda, R. F., & Nordenberg, D., Williamson, D. F., Spitz, A. M., Edwards, V., Koss, M.P., & Marks, J.S., (1998). Relationship of childhood abuse and household dysfunction to many of the leading causes of death in adults: The adverse childhood experiences (ACE) study. American Journal of Preventive Medicine, 14(4), 245-258.

20 Centers for Disease Control at http://www.cdc.gov/violencepre-vention/acestudy/about.html

21 Center for the Developing Child, Harvard University. Developingchild.harvard.edu. Key Concepts

22 Bremner, J. D. (2002). Does stress damage the brain?. New York, NY: W. W. Norton & Company, Inc.

23 While the ACE pyramid actually lists only emotional, psychological, and social problems, other researchers have found that it also leads to spiritual problems. Therefore I have added spiritual problems at this level.

24 Ganje-Fling, M., Veach, P. M., Kuang, H., & Houg, B., (2000). Effects of childhood sexual abuse on client spiritual well-being. *Counseling and Values*, 44(2), 84.

25 Eurelings-Bontekoe, E. H. M., Hekman-Van Steeg, J., & Verschuur, M. J. (2005). The association between personality, attachment, psychological distress, church denomination and the God concept among a non-clinical sample. *Mental Health, Religion & Culture*, 8(2), 141-154.

26 International Journal of Obesity (2002) 26, 1075 – 1082. doi:10.1038=sj.ijo.0802038

27 Williamson, DF, Thompson, TJ, Anda, RF, Dietz, WH, and Felitti, V. (2002). Body weight and obesity in adults and self-reported abuse in childhood. International Journal of Obesity. 26, 1075–1082.

28 U.S. Department of Health and Human Services, 2014

29 NY Times. The Smoking Divide (2014) retrieved from http://www.nytimes.com/interactive/2014/03/25/us/smoking-rate-map.html?_r=0

30 Felitti, V. J. (2004). The origins of addiction: Evidence from the Adverse Childhood Experiences study. Retrieved from http://www.acestudy.org/files/OriginsofAddiction.pdf

31 Duran et al, 2004.

32 Eurelings-Bontekoe, E. H. M., Hekman-Van Steeg, J., & Verschuur,

M. J. (2005). The association between personality, attachment, psychological distress, church denomination and the God concept among a non-clinical sample. *Mental Health, Religion & Culture,* 8(2), 141-154.

33 Johannes Kepler, author of modern astronomy; 1571-1630

Chapter 2: It's Not Your Fault, but it is Your Problem!

34 Felitti, V. J. (2004). The Origins of Addiction: Evidence from the Adverse Childhood Experiences study. Retrieved from http://www.acestudy.org/files/OriginsofAddiction.pdf

35 This concept of trauma development in the brain/mind was, to my knowledge, first espoused by Jesse Collins in his training on Etiotropic Trauma Management/Trauma Resolution therapy. I've modified it, adapted it, and personalized it with my own theories and ideas. This should not be confused with his ETM/TRT model and is not an attempt to plagiarize or pirate his ideas, but to build on them and move the science of trauma counseling forward.

36 Boundless, a concept-based learning system online is a good resource for learning more. https://www.boundless.com/psychology/textbooks/boundless-psychology-textbook/biological-foundations-of-psychology-3/structure-and-function-of-the-brain-35/the-limbic-system-154-12689/

37 Herman, J. L. (1997). Trauma and Recovery: *The aftermath of violence—from domestic abuse to political terror.* New York, NY: BasicBooks.

38 Quote By Billy Graham. (n.d.). Quotery. Retrieved from http://www.quotery.com/quotes/prayer-is-simply-a-two-way-conversation-between-you-and/

39 Foster, R. J. (2009-10-13). Prayer - 10th Anniversary Edition: Finding the Heart's True Home (p. 10). HarperCollins. Kindle Edition.

40 IBID

41 IBID

Chapter 3: Embrace Your Weakness

42 TerKeurst, L. (2014). The Best Yes: Making Wise Decisions in the Midst of Endless Demands. Thomas Nelson.

43 Brené Brown, (2012). *Daring Greatly*. Penguin Group.

44 Amplified Bible (AMP). (1954, 1958, 1962, 1964, 1965, 1987). LaHabra, CA, the Lockman Foundation.

Chapter 4: Stop Trying to Fix Yourself!

45 Schaefer, M. (2012) 9 Lies You Hear in Church: #3. God Never Gives You More Than You Can Bear. Kay Spiritual Life Center. Retrieved from http://www.aumethodists.org/worship/sermons/2012-fall/9-lies-you-hear-in-church-3-god-never-gives-you-more-than-you-can-bear/

Chapter 5: Navigating the Wilderness of Grief

46 Wallace, L. (2014) Indifference is power. Retrieved from http://aeon.co/magazine/philosophy/why-stoicism-is-one-of-the-best-mind-hacks-ever/. Interestingly written on Christmas Eve

47 Elgot, J. and Sommers, J. (2015). Holocaust Denial Worries Historians and Religious Leaders As Survivors Dwindle. The Huffington Post U.K. Retrieved from http://www.huffingtonpost.co.uk/2015/01/29/holocaust-denial_n_6571934.html

48 Ridley, L. (2015). The Holocaust's Forgotten Victims: The 5 Million Non-Jewish People Killed By the Nazis. The Huffington Post U.K. Retrieved 1/5/2016 from http://www.huffingtonpost.co.uk/2015/01/26/non-jewish-holocaust-victims_n_6500948.html?utm_hp_ref=uk

49 Vogel, Edward K., Trafton, Drew. (2008). Why do we forget things? Scientific American. Retrieved from http://www.scientificamerican.com/article/why-do-we-forget-things/

50 Nils Hadziselimovic, N. et al. (2014). Forgetting is regulated via Musashi-mediated translational control of the Arp2/3 complex. Cell. Vol 156:6. Pps. 1153-1166.

51 Yehuda R1, Kahana B, Schmeidler J, Southwick SM, Wilson S, Giller EL. (1995). Impact of cumulative lifetime trauma and recent stress

on current posttraumatic stress disorder symptoms in holocaust survivors. Am J Psychiatry. 152(12):1815-8.

52 This concept of emotion stacking in the brain/mind I first heard from Jesse Collins in his training on Etiotropic Trauma Management/Trauma Resolution therapy. However, this is a universal concept and I've tried to explain it in my own way. I also explained it in my first book, *Stop Treating Symptoms and Start Resolving Trauma!* In which I referenced Mr. Collins extensively.

53 The Free Dictionary, Medical Dictionary, n.d.

54 McAdams, D. P. (2006). The person: A new introduction to personality psychology. (4th ed.). Hoboken, NJ: Wiley.

55 Wallace, L. (2014) Indifference is power. Retrieved from http://aeon.co/magazine/philosophy/why-stoicism-is-one-of-the-best-mind-hacks-ever/. Interestingly written on Christmas Eve.

56 Wallace, L. (2014) Indifference is power. Retrieved from http://aeon.co/magazine/philosophy/why-stoicism-is-one-of-the-best-mind-hacks-ever/. Interestingly written on Christmas Eve.

57 O'Neil, S. H. (2012). SBIRT: Re-conceptualizing our understanding of substance use problems. Slides from SBIRT presentation.

58 O'Neil, S. (2013). SBIRT: Re-conceptualizing Our Understanding of Substance Use Problems. A PowerPoint Presentation

59 IBID

60 Foundation for a Drug Free World. Retrieved from http://www.drugfreeworld.org/drugfacts/alcohol/short-term-long-term-effects.html

61 National Institute on Alcohol Abuse and Alcoholism. (2015). Retrieved from http://pubs.niaaa.nih.gov/publications/Practitioner/pocketguide/pocket_guide2.htm

62 Norton, Merle. Lecture.

63 U.S. Department of Health & Human Services National Institutes Of Health National Institute on Alcohol Abuse and Alcoholism. (2005). Helping patients who drink too much a clinician's guide.

Retrieved from http://www.integration.samhsa.gov/clinical-practice/Helping_Patients_Who_Drink_Too_Much.pdf

64 NLT (The New Living Translation). (2004). the Holy Bible New Living Translation. Carol Stream, IL. Tyndale House Publishers.

65 Felitti, V. J. (2004). The Origins of Addiction: Evidence from the Adverse Childhood Experiences study. Retrieved from http://www.acestudy.org/files/OriginsofAddiction.pdf

66 Ivey, A.E. and Zalaquett, C.P. (2011). Neuroscience and counseling: Central issue for social justice leaders. Journal for Social Action in Counseling and Psychology; vol 3, number 1.

67 Prochaska JO, DiClemente CC, Norcross JC. (1992).In search of how people change. Am Psychol, 47:1102-4.

68 Felitti, V. J. (2004). The Origins of Addiction: Evidence from the Adverse Childhood Experiences study. Retrieved from http://www.acestudy.org/files/OriginsofAddiction.pdf

Chapter 6: Partnering for Healing

69 McSpadden, W.J. (1907). Stories from Chaucer. Retold from the Canterbury Tales. Thomas Y. Crowel & Co, New York.

70 Felitti, V. (2011). The Relationship of Adverse Childhood Experiences to Adult Health: Turning gold into lead. Retrieved from http://www.albertafamilywellness.org/resources/video/origins-addiction

71 Smedes, Lewis. (1993). Healing The Shame We Don't Deserve. Preface. San Francisco: Harper Collins Publishers

72 Brown, B. (2012). TED Talk- Listening to Shame. Retrieved from https://www.youtube.com/watch?v=L0ifUM1DYKg

73 Siegel, D. J. (2010). Mindsight: The New Science of Personal Transformation. Bantam Books.

74 Brown, B. (2015). Daring Greatly: How the Courage to Be Vulnerable Transforms the Way We Live, Love, Parent, and Lead. Avery Publishers.

75 Wiseman, T. (1996). A concept analysis of empathy. Journal of Advanced Nursing 23, 1162-1167.

76 Henry, M. (1997) Mathew Henry's Commentary on the Whole Bible. TN. Thomas Nelson.

77 IBID

78 Osborne, G., R. (Ed). (1997). John. The IVP New Testament Commentary Series. IL, Intervarsity Press.

79 Brown, B. (2010). The Gifts of Imperfection: Let Go of Who You Think You're Supposed to be and Embrace Who You Are. Hazelden Publishers.

Chapter 7: Moving from Faith to Hope

80 Olff, M., Koeter, M., W., J., E. Van Haaften, H., Kersten, P., H., and Gersons, B., P., R., (2005). Impact of a foot and mouth disease crisis on post-traumatic stress symptoms in farmers. The British Journal of Psychiatry, 186: 165 - 166.

81 Mol, S., S., L, Arntz, A., Metsemakers, J., F., M., Dinant, G-J, Vilters-Van Montfort, P., A., P., and Knottnerus, J., A. (2005). Symptoms of post-traumatic stress disorder after non-traumatic events: Evidence from an open population study. The British Journal of Psychiatry, 2005; 186: 494 - 499.

82 Herman, J. L. (1997). Trauma and recovery; the aftermath of violence--from domestic abuse to political terror. New York, NY: BasicBooks.

83 2015 Merriam-Webster, Incorporated

84 IBID

85 View this scene at https://www.youtube.com/watch?v=xFntFdEGgws

86 Palmer, L. D. (2014). Growing hope. Spirituality and Health. Retrieved from spiritualityhealth.com

87 IBID

88 Navidian, A. & Bahari, F. (2014). The impact of mixed, hope and

forgiveness-focused marital counselling on interpersonal cognitive distortions of couples filing for divorce. Journal of Psychiatric & Mental Health Nursing. Vol. 21 Issue 7.

89 Scioli, A., Samor, C. M., Campbell, T. L., Chamberlin, C. M., Lapointe, A. B., Macleod, A. R., & Mclenon, J. (1997). A prospective study of hope, optimism, and health. Psychological Reports, 81(3), 723-733. doi: 10.2466/pr0.1997.81.3.723.

90 Chang, E. C. (2003). A critical appraisal and extension of hope theory in middle-aged men and women: Is it important to distinguish agency and pathways components? Journal of Social and Clinical Psychology, 22(2), 121-143.

91 O'Hara, D. J. (2011). Psychotherapy and the dialectics of hope and despair. Counselling Psychology Quarterly. Vol. 24 Issue 4.

Made in the USA
Columbia, SC
06 December 2018